MEXICO CITY

MEXICO CITY

ALEJANDRO ROSAS

ILLUSTRATIONS BY KEVIN CUEVAS

TRANSLATION BY THOMAS McGOWAN EDWARDS
AND ANDREA GÁLVEZ DE AGUINAGA

Tinta Books / Trinity University Press
San Antonio, Texas

Tinta Books, an imprint of Trinity University Press
San Antonio, Texas 78212

Book design by Nostra Ediciones

ISBN 978-1-59534-282-9 paperback

Trinity University Press strives to produce its books using methods and materials in an environmentally sensitive manner. We favor working with manufacturers that practice sustainable management of all natural resources, produce paper using recycled stock, and manage forests with the best possible practices for people, biodiversity, and sustainability. The press is a member of the Green Press Initiative, a nonprofit program dedicated to supporting publishers in their efforts to reduce their impacts on endangered forests, climate change, and forest-dependent communities. The paper used in this publication meets the minimum requirements of the American National Standard for Information Sciences—Permanence of Paper for Printed Library Materials, ANSI 39.48-1992.

CIP data on file at the Library of Congress

27 26 25 24 23 | 5 4 3 2 1

Contents

The Sixteenth Century

How a city is born

And he wasn't wrong . . .

On August 13, 1521, after a sixty-five-day siege, Tenochtitlan, the legendary capital of the Mexican empire, succumbed to the onslaught of thousands of Tlaxcalans, Huejotzingas, and other indigenous groups, who had allied with some twelve hundred Spanish soldiers, to end the yoke of the people of the sun.

No stone was left standing. Hernán Cortés struggled through the rubble of stately homes and palaces that had amazed him in November 1519. Hundreds of corpses covered the flooded dirt streets.

The city was left in pitiful, smoky ruins. It was difficult to breathe the polluted air. There was no food, and the drinking water supply had been interrupted because the aqueduct had been destroyed at the beginning of the siege. That August 13, 1521, Tenochtitlan was practically uninhabitable.

Cortés ordered the cleanup work to begin, and the corpses were buried immediately to prevent an epidemic. The work would take several months. While his men worked in the city, Cortés knew that sooner or later he had to make a decision that would mark history: Should he found the new city on the same island where the ruins of Tenochtitlan lay, or was it better to build it on solid ground? While he pondered, the conquistador decided to settle in a town on the southern shore of the lake—Coyoacán, which he called "his beloved village."

Just as with Villa Rica de la Vera Cruz in 1519, Cortés organized in Coyoacán the first city hall of the Valley of Mexico, which was responsible for granting land to all the conquerors to guarantee the settlement of what would be the capital of New Spain. In Coyoacán, Mexico City was officially born.

As the weeks passed, the islet recovered its dignity. The water returned through acequias (irrigation canals), and the air recovered its legendary purity.

Even so, the Spanish considered only three sites with the right conditions on the mainland to found the Spanish city: Tacuba, Texcoco, and Coyoacán.

But in the first months of 1522, Cortés made the momentous decision to establish the new city on the remains of the indigenous city. The capital of New Spain would rise over Mexico-Tenochtitlan, and the conqueror prophesied that he would attain the greatness of times past.

In the eyes of his peers and members of the city council, Cortés's decision was preposterous: the new city would be built on an islet with only three accesses to the mainland, acequias that crossed the city on all sides, and an outside drinking fountain, all surrounded by a large lake and strategically vulnerable—as demonstrated by Cortés himself during the siege. What advantages did it have over Coyoacán or Texcoco?

The reasons for settling on the islet were based not on urban logic but on political significance. The vision Cortés had was very clear: Tenochtitlan had not been an ordinary city but the center of the Mexica universe; all peoples knew of the imperial capital's existence and either by will or force respected and paid tribute to it. Abandoning the islet could lead to its transformation into a bastion of indigenous resistance against the Spanish presence. Cortés wanted to build a city on this site that united both universes—the Spanish and the indigenous—and thus safeguard its greatness. The odds were against him, but he was not wrong.

The eagle and the serpent

According to the chronicles, Huitzilopochtli appeared to the lords of Aztlán to order them to look for a new place to settle. The right site would be marked by an eagle perched on a nopal cactus. Thus in 1116 began a pilgrimage that would end in 1325, when the Aztecs found the sign on a small and inhospitable islet in the middle of a lake in the Valley of Mexico. There they founded their new city, Mexico-Tenochtitlan.

This famous mythical sign became the symbol of the Mexica people, the symbol of the empire, the symbol of Tenochtitlan, and managed to overcome time to insert itself into the collective imagination of New Spain during three hundred years of domination, ultimately becoming the national coat of arms of an independent Mexico.

Barely two years after the fall of Tenochtitlan, in 1523, King Carlos V granted a coat of arms to Mexico City. Its background was blue like the sign of the great lagoon the city was built on. In the middle stood a golden castle with three stone bridges. Two lions stood on lateral bridges on their hind legs, touching the castle with their claws as a sign of victory. The coat of arms was surrounded by nopal cactus leaves symbolizing the place where the city was founded, according to Mexica tradition.

> The bridges of Carlos V's coat of arms were broken to symbolize that the ancient city had been defeated.

Neither the Spanish nor the indigenous chiefs liked the coat of arms granted by Carlos V. The authorities could not refuse it, but they contrived to establish another. The new emblem lacked the gravitas of the insignia that was placed above the coat of arms, and the city council decided to stamp it with a more appropriate symbol reflecting recent history: an eagle perched on a nopal cactus. Thus the Mexica coat of arms prevailed over Spanish heraldry.

Beginning in the middle of the sixteenth century, the people of Mexico City started to identify with the Mexica coat of arms to such an extent that in 1642 Viceroy Juan de Palafox realized that it was more recognized than the Spanish coat of arms, and he ordered the removal of the eagle that adorned the main fountain of Mexico City.

By the eighteenth century, however, the eagle and the nopal cactus were already part of daily life in New Spain and were disseminated in municipal institutions, academies, public buildings, religious paintings, artifacts, history books, and personal objects. New Spain had become Mexicanized.

The shield, of course, was a way not to claim autonomy or independence for New Spain over the crown but to grant Mexico City a predominant place compared to other cities of New Spain. The coat of arms of New Spain's capital would become the entire territory's once independence was realized.

What about the snake?

No document, codex, or painting mentions the serpent in the original legend of the founding of Tenochtitlan. In some Mexica illustrations, such as the *Codex Mendoza*, an eagle is shown, while the *Codex Ramírez* refers to Huitzilopochtli ordering the Aztecs to find a majestic bird perched on a nopal cactus. The chronicler Chimalpahin mentions the eagle devouring something but does not say what it is.

The serpent appears on the indigenous coat of arms many years after Mexico's conquest as a reference to evil, in accordance with the Christian tradition. It arose from an incorrect translation of the *Crónica Mexicayotl* by Fernando de Alvarado Tezozómoc.

A Nahuatl phrase meaning "the snake hisses" was translated as "the serpent is destroyed." Based on this, Fray Diego Durán reinterpreted the legend so that the eagle represented good and the snake represented evil and sin, according to Christian and Hispanic tradition. He used this version for the first time in 1582 to illustrate his *History of the Indies of New Spain*. This was how the eagle devouring the snake began to appear indistinctly on the indigenous coat of arms and as a symbol for Mexico City, finally becoming the national coat of arms.

The first city layout

By the beginning of 1523, many of Tenochtitlan's buildings had disappeared. Several were still visible in the space where the great teocalli (temple) stood.

Toward the east of the island, in the so-called shelter of San Lázaro, the Spanish were about to finish the shipyard fortress, where they docked boats that came to

the city from the lake. Cortés ordered its construction while Tenochtitlan was being cleaned up.

In the shipyards, Cortés docked the thirteen brigantines used during the siege of Tenochtitlan. The building stored equipment for their ships and functioned as an arsenal. In the event of an indigenous revolt, the Spanish could take refuge in the shipyards and flee the island in the brigantines.

Cortés entrusted Spanish master builder Alonso García Bravo with the first layout of the new city. Tenochtitlan's layout was similar to many European cities: a quadrangular center, where the great teocalli and other temples were located, was divided by four principal carriageways in the direction of the four cardinal points flanked by important buildings: temples, palaces, and manor houses. This same layout was used to design the new city of Mexico.

Following García Bravo's specifications, the initial layout formed a large square with an area about 145 hectares smaller than the indigenous city.

The north side of the Spanish city was bounded by present-day Calle República de Colombia, and the south side by present-day Avenida José María Izazaga; the east side reached to present-day Anillo de Circunvalación; and the west side was bounded by present-day Avenida Lázaro Cárdenas. The waterways prevented the walling of the city, but it was arranged so that only the Spanish lived there. The Indians were grouped into neighborhoods, as in olden days, behind acequias that formed the natural boundaries of the initial layout.

Cortés had had his eye on two magnificent constructions since he first set foot in the Mexica city in 1519—the palace of Moctezuma, where the National Palace is now located, and the Palace of Axayacatl, where the current Nacional Monte de Piedad is located. As chief of chiefs, Cortés kept them, and this was ratified by the king of Spain in 1529.

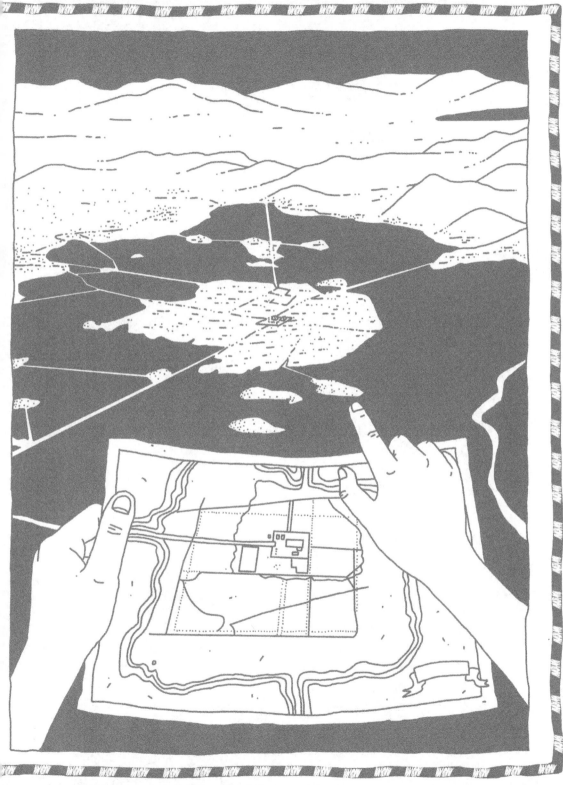

Stone upon stone

Once construction of the shipyards was finished, Cortés and his men left Coyoacán and moved to the island, where he stayed and established the capital of New Spain. To populate the city, land was distributed as a reward for services rendered. Each conqueror received two plots of land within the limits of the layout (one plot was equivalent to 1,756 square meters), one for participating in the conquest and the other for being a neighbor, which implied that they must establish their residence and remain there for at least ten years.

To ensure that the city grew in an orderly fashion, in 1524 the city council ordered people who owned lots to clean them up and fence them by Christmas 1524 under penalty of forfeiting them.

For their part, the indigenous people rebuilt their houses outside the layout, where the Spanish were prohibited from building unless otherwise authorized.

The first houses were built with tezontle stone and materials extracted from remains of indigenous palaces and temples. García Bravo designed flat straight streets, and as such, in the early 1530s, the city council ordered demolition of those works "that did not respect the alignment of the streets and not to build the façades of lime and stone." "They are so wide that two carriages can comfortably go through them in opposite directions, and three at a time," Francisco Cervantes de Salazar wrote in his work

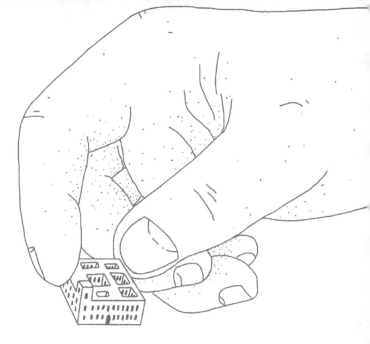

Mexico in 1554. Of Calle Tacuba, the oldest street in the city, he wrote, "How the mind rejoices and delights the eye, the look of this street! How long and wide! How straight! How flat! And completely paved, so that in the rainy season it does not become muddy and dirty . . . the water runs on top through its channel, so that it is more pleasant."

Thousands of indigenous people from nearby towns participated in the construction of New Spain's capital. Friar Toribio Benavente, also known as "Motolinía," wrote that construction of the great Mexico City required more men than were used to erect the temple of Jerusalem in the time of King Solomon.

Together with the civilian constructions, charitable public establishments began to take shape within the layout. In 1524 Cortés founded the famous Hospital de Jesús —which continues to provide services to this day, and where his remains are buried.

The following year, the establishment of inns was allowed, where bread, meat, and wine were sold to Spaniards looking for accommodation while they were building. In 1526 two lots were granted to found the hermitage of San Cosme. One more lot was granted to Master Pedro and Benito Bejel in the Plaza Mayor (main square) to establish a school of dance, "because this ennobled the city." In 1527 a tannery was established.

In the years immediately following the conquest, inhabitants of the new city lived uneasily. Although the alliances with the indigenous people allowed for peaceful coexistence, the indigenous population was superior in number to the Spanish, and although a rebellion was unlikely, there was always the possibility.

Some provisions made by the First Hearing (1528–30) showed the conquerors' fear. The Spaniards were forbidden, under penalty of death, to sell, grant, exchange, or even lend to the indigenous population "horse or mare, due to the inconvenience that could result from Indians riding a horse." Prohibition extended to weapons. Under no circumstances could indigenous people learn to use them.

Calle Tacuba, where the Spaniards fled during the battle of La Noche Triste (Night of Sorrows) in 1520, was the first to be populated. All the lots on the street were occupied between 1524 and 1527, from the Plaza Mayor to San Juan de Letran (Avenida Lázaro Cárdenas).

In the stretch that runs from the present-day street, from Avenida Isabel la Católica to the Parish of Santa Veracruz, which is in front of the north side of the central mall, Calle Tacuba was residential. Beyond the church were country houses and orchards. At the point called the Tlaxpana, Tacuba connected from the left with the road to Chapultepec (today Circuito Interior).

Houses were built next to each other, with towers and battlements for defense that reflected Spanish fear. "From its solidity," Cervantes de Salazar wrote years later, "anyone would say that they were not houses but fortresses. . . . That is why it was convenient to build them at the beginning, when there were many enemies, when the city could not be protected, encircling it with towers and walls."

This way of building made strategic sense. In case of danger, the Spanish could reach the mainland quickly or defend themselves from their own buildings. The gradual miscegenation ended, however, removing any threat of insurrection, and around 1550 the shipyard fortress was in a dilapidated state as safety finally reigned in New Spain's capital.

Plaza Mayor

It wasn't a square of wide-open spaces. It wasn't the politicized public square where more than a hundred thousand people would congregate regularly at the end of the twentieth century. It was by no means the "main square," with its solitary flagpole.

Mexico City's Plaza Mayor was born as the political, economic, and social center of New Spain. For centuries it was the heart that beat unceasingly, giving life to the capital of the viceroyalty. It was the place where night and day merged into one continuous movement, where voices did not stop and power found its origin and destiny.

Its beauty was born of the daily chaos of the grape harvest, disorderly movement, the calls of the town criers, the passing horses and carriages, the barges that docked in front of the city council, the Indians who came from all regions to sell their products, the religious processions, the sound of the water falling in the fountains, the acts of faith, the pillory erected in its center, and the judicial, land, and political affairs that were administered by the Royal Houses.

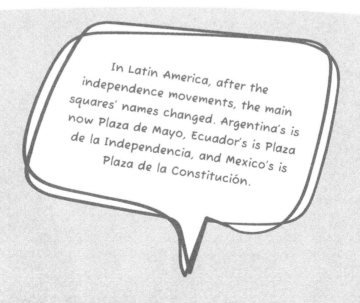

In Latin America, after the independence movements, the main squares' names changed. Argentina's is now Plaza de Mayo, Ecuador's is Plaza de la Independencia, and Mexico's is Plaza de la Constitución.

In the mid-sixteenth century, Cervantes de Salazar described the bustling main square of New Spain's capital through the characters of his work, *Mexico in 1554*:

> Zuazo: We are already in the plaza. Look closely see if you've ever encountered another that is equal in grandeur and majesty.
>
> Alfaro: I certainly don't remember any, nor do I think in both worlds can two the same be found. My God! How flat and extensive! What joy! How adorned with tall and proud buildings, for the four winds! What regularity! What beauty! What an arrangement and setting!
>
> Zuazo: It is made so wide so that it is not necessary to sell anything anywhere else. . . . Here they celebrate fairs or markets; auctions are held, and all kinds of goods can be found; here come merchants from all over this land with their goods, and finally, the best in Spain comes to this square.

For many years the Plaza Mayor had a rectangular shape. In 1524 ten plots of land (17,560 square meters) were allocated for construction of the first cathedral of Mexico (although it wasn't granted the title of cathedral until 1547). The temple initially occupied almost half the square; its main entrance faced west, in the direction of present-day Monte de Piedad.

Construction of the first cathedral allowed the center of the new capital to have two plazas: the Plaza Mayor, as it is known today, and the Plaza del Marqués in front of Monte de Piedad. There was one more square, known as Plaza del Volador, located at the site currently occupied by the Supreme Court building.

The Plaza Mayor reflected the Spanish squares of the time. On one side was the temple; on another, the town hall, butcher shop, and jail; and on another, the seat of political power and the doorways of flower merchants.

Street commerce had taken root as early as the 1530s. Stalls were set up daily and removed only on special occasions, such as Paseo del Pendón (procession of the banner), which commemorated the fall of Tenochtitlan and founding of Mexico City, or the arrival of the new viceroy, as well as some ceremonies, processions, and religious rituals.

The disorderly growth of market stalls in the Plaza Mayor worried the viceroy, Don Luis de Velasco II, who, in 1609, ordered that vendors could not have stores in the plaza "except by appointment of the Mayor and representative of the City Council, so that the square has the appropriate layout and that they pay the corresponding amount for the position and site that is given to him."

The first bullfight in New Spain took place on June 24, 1526—Saint John's Day—to liven up the religious festival and welcome Hernán Cortés, who was returning from his expedition to Las Hibueras (present-day Honduras). From then on they were organized when the coronations of the Spanish kings swore an oath upon accession to the throne, when the viceroys entered the city on holy days.

The first bullfighters were the Spanish nobles themselves, who liked risking their lives. The bullfights took place in four places—Plaza Mayor, Plaza del Volador, Plaza del Marqués (the space formed between the Metropolitan Cathedral and Monte de Piedad), and Plaza Guardiola (in front of the House of Tiles at the start of Avenida Madero downtown).

How to rule

It is said that the one who hits first hits twice, and Cortés provided the best example of that adage. While the Spanish crown was deciding how to administer and organize its colonies in the Americas, King Charles I of Spain and V of Germany granted Cortés the political, military, and judicial powers of the new kingdom, and the conquistador became the first ruler of Mexico after the conquest.

In 1526, after his failed expedition to the Hibueras, Cortés returned to Mexico City to find that the king had stripped him of his power, granting him only a title—marquis of the valley of Oaxaca. To lessen the blow, the king modestly granted him twenty thousand vassals for his service.

The intrigues of his enemies were successful: the conqueror was displaced and his place taken by unscrupulous people. King Carlos V thought that if several men instead of one governed via an audience, the new territories would be better managed. He was wrong. The two committees that ruled

New Spain between 1526 and 1535 were a failure. After the latter, the king divided his domains into viceroyalties, each headed by a viceroy appointed by the king as his direct representative.

The first viceroy of New Spain, Antonio de Mendoza, arrived in 1535 with very clear orders: to keep an eye on the Catholic cult, distribute the land among the conquerors, oversee the evangelization of the Indians, and take care that they received dignified treatment.

During his administration, the first printing press in the American continent was established, which influenced the founding of the Royal and Pontifical University of Mexico. The viceroy also ordered the founding of the mint and promoted the creation of the College of the Holy Cross of Tlatelolco for cacique Indians.

The second viceroy, Don Luis de Velasco, undertook numerous works in Mexico City that had begun under the previous viceroy's mandate. Thus, in 1553 he inaugurated the Royal and Pontifical University of Mexico, which became a hotbed of culture and knowledge for New Spain's youth. In 1562 he decided to buy the property that used to be Moctezuma's palace from Martín Cortés, the son of Hernán Cortés (who died in 1547). From then on, the viceroys inhabited the building that was previously known as the Viceregal Palace and is known today as the National Palace.

Everyday Life

By the end of the sixteenth century, Mexico City had its own personality; it was recognized as the great capital of the viceroyalty and enjoyed a unique architecture completely different from the pre-Hispanic era. The city became renowned for its grandeur, similar to that of Tenochtitlan a century earlier.

Plaza Mayor underwent some important transformations. The cathedral built in the 1520s was humble, and the king of Spain ordered construction of a new cathedral worthy of Mexico City's greatness. A few centuries after the foundation stone was laid in 1573, the cathedral would be completed in 1813.

The streets leading to Plaza Mayor began to have their own dynamics. The main ones were Calle San Francisco and Calle Plateros (today Avenida Madero), which started from San Juan de Letran (today Eje Central) and ended at Plaza Mayor. The first section was named after San Francisco, one of the most impressive convents in all of Hispanic America. The section known as Plateros housed and honored the most important jewelers of New Spain, whose creations of gold and silver were true works of art.

Another important street, known today as Avenida 16 de Septiembre, was one of the few waterways that remained open until the eighteenth century. One had to travel through it in a canoe. Through its channel ran the palace acequia, one of the city's seven great acequias, which is why it was also known as the Acequia Real (royal irrigation canal). Along it were several businesses, and its name changed on differ-

ent stretches: Tlapaleros, El Refugio, Coliseo Viejo, Colegio de Niñas (one of the first theaters), and Callejón de Dolores.

On Tacuba were all kinds of business tradesmen: carpenters, blacksmiths, locksmiths, shoemakers, weavers, barbers, bakers, painters, chiselers, tailors, bootmakers, armorers, boat builders, crossbowmen, swordsmiths, biscuit makers, fishmongers, and turners.

In Plaza Mayor there were also the Portal de Mercaderes in front of the Viceroy's Palace and the Portal de las Flores on the square's south side, where trade was also given free rein. People went about their daily lives according to schedules set by the chimes of the temple bells.

The presence of both the viceroy and the archbishop at processions or religious festivals was obligatory. Next to the Viceroy's Palace was the Archbishop's Palace and the mint.

In 1530 Pope Clement VII issued a bull that created the archbishopric of Mexico. Three years later, Carlos V established that the "houses were bishops' houses, for Friar Juan of Zumárraga and later his successors, to live and dwell in them forever."

According to Motolinía, the Archbishop's Palace was built "in the very place where the devil had his temple," referring to the site where the Templo Mayor, with its shrine dedicated to Huitzilopochtli, was built. But it was not all happiness for the archbishops who lived there; the water supply was a permanent headache. The original pipeline, laid in the time of Zumárraga, broke soon afterward, and water didn't flow again until the beginning of the seventeenth century.

The foundry was established on one of the properties purchased by Zumárraga. The first bells to sound in the temples of Mexico were created inside the Archbishop's Palace, under the bishop's supervision, from an artillery piece gifted by Hernán Cortés. Construction was completed by 1554. At the end of the eighteenth century, a large part of the palace was restored and remodeled into its present form.

After the conquest, the Spanish who began to settle Mexico City would stroll in Chapultepec forest on the weekends, and in 1528 the city council authorized Juan Díaz del Real to "sell bread, wine and other supplies there, to those who were going to relax." Viceroy Don Luis de Velasco dedicated the forest to Emperor Charles V. He ordered it to be fenced to prevent hunters from wiping out animal species, and he released sight hounds in the surrounding area—in Mexico only the Mexican hairless (*xoloitzcuintle*) was known—which soon spread. The viceroys recognized the benefits of the place, and on top of the hill over the remains of a pre-Hispanic shrine they authorized construction of a hermitage dedicated to Saint Francis Xavier and planned the construction of a recreational residence.

One of Mexico City's oldest and most traditional promenades is the Alameda Central (central grove), built in 1592 by order of Viceroy Luis of Velasco. It derives its name from poplars planted in the area. Over the years it became the obligatory stroll for the capital's high society, a place for recreation, amusement, and entertainment. Such was its beauty that around 1775 Viceroy Antonio María Bucareli ordered that music be performed on Sundays and holidays for the delight of visitors. But it was not until 1892, under the government of Porfirio Díaz, that electric lights were installed in the grove; inside was a skating rink where one could have refreshments or admire the

sculptures that adorned the park, such as the Benito Juárez Hemicycle.

During the viceregal period, on the grove's west side, was the Inquisition's execution site, a gloomy place where those sentenced to death were devoured by fire. The grove continues to be a meeting place today, and at Christmas it has become customary for parents to take their children and have their picture taken with the Wise Men.

By the end of the century, the Jesuits had made their presence felt with the College of San Ildefonso, La Profesa (Church of San Felipe Neri), and the San Pedro y San Pablo College, another Jesuit academic institution of excellence. On Tepeyac Hill, one of the first shrines dedicated to the Virgin of Guadalupe was already visible, like the one dedicated to the Virgin of the Remedies on the city's outskirts.

Two virgins in New Spain's capital

Since 1531, with the story of the apparition of the mother of God on Tepeyac Hill, where the Aztecs venerated the goddess Tonantzin ("our little mother"), there had been no doubt: she was accepted and respected by all social strata. The fact that the Virgin had shown herself to a humble Indian, Juan Diego, was a divine sign that made the kingdom of New Spain a "chosen" people.

The image of the dark-skinned Virgin won the hearts of creoles and indigenous people, although the Spanish preferred the Virgin of the Remedies. Devotion to her developed naturally and grew from 1531 onward, but it was not until April 27, 1737, that she was declared the patron saint of Mexico City. Ten years later she became the patron saint of New Spain.

The other Virgin arrived first. According to tradition, Juan Rodríguez de Villafuerte, one of Hernán Cortés's men, brought a statue of the Virgin of the Remedies "for solace."

Upon arriving in Tenochtitlan, Cortés ordered Villa-fuerte to place the image on an altar in the Templo Mayor where human sacrifices had been made. It was displayed there for a few weeks until war broke out, after which nothing more was heard of the small wooden statue.

During the defeat of La Noche Triste, on June 30, 1520, Cortés had to hastily withdraw from Mexico-Tenochtitlan. Exhausted and demoralized, he and his men reached a small hill in front of the town of Tlacopan and spent the night there. It is said that the Virgin appeared accompanied by Santiago (Saint James), the patron saint of Spain, and the dejected conquerors found a haven of peace, trusting that the mother of God would lead them to final victory. A year later, Mexico-Tenochtitlan fell.

Around 1540 an Indian cacique, Juan de Águila, was walking near the town of Tacuba and saw the Lady in heaven, "who with a sensitive voice said to him: 'My son, look for me in that town.'" Shortly afterward, under a maguey cactus, he found the old wooden statuette that had been missing since 1520. Around 1575 the temple was completed, and her image was venerated.

The people appealed to the Virgin of the Remedies in times of drought and during epidemics, like measles. For years her image traveled the Mexico-Tacuba road to protect the people from terrible epidemics, floods, and tremors that from time to time reminded inhabitants of the city that nature had no religion. In colorful and multitudinous processions, the ecclesiastical and civil authorities—including the viceroy himself—removed the Virgin from her sanctuary in the city's sentry boxes and placed her for months in the Cathedral of Mexico City.

When calamities did not subside, not even with the intercession of the Virgin of the Remedies, the authorities turned to the Virgin of Guadalupe as a last resort. This caused some unease among the people, as it seemed an insult to turn to the dark-skinned Virgin as a second option. But happiness prevailed when the people could observe the Virgin of Guadalupe close up at the front of a procession.

The rivalry between the two virgins continued until the War of Independence (1810–21). The Virgin of Guadalupe became the banner of the insurgency, and the Virgin of the Remedies became the flag of the royalists. In the end, the dark-skinned Virgin emerged victorious.

The situation is very serious

During the sixteenth century, the epidemics that ravaged the entire territory made it more difficult for the indigenous peoples than for any other group. The epidemics were so severe that the native population almost disappeared.

Some diseases, such as smallpox, were unknown in America. The epidemic broke out between 1519 and 1520 in Tenochtitlan and took Cuitláhuac, the last Aztec *tlatoani* (ruler), to his grave. The Indians suffered measles in 1531, chickenpox in 1538, plague in 1545, and mumps in 1550, but the worst of them all was cocoliztli in 1576, which, although difficult to identify, caused the deaths of two million people. It is said that after that epidemic, the phrase "la cosa está del cocol" was coined, meaning that the situation was very serious.

There was no shortage of social scandals in New Spain's capital, the biggest of which occurred around 1563 when Martín Cortés, son of Hernán Cortés and Juana Zúñiga, attempted to make the viceroyalty independent and set himself up as its king. But his actions were ambiguous, and he played both sides: before New Spain authorities, he swore absolute loyalty to the king, and among the conspirators he encouraged the rebellion without daring to lead it.

This led to the conspiracy being discovered in 1565. Arrests followed, and the authorities publicly executed two of the most active leaders: Alonso de Ávila and Gil González Benavides de Ávila. Martín Cortés never confessed to the crime of rebellion, but he was tortured and banished, and faced the death penalty if he returned.

The Seventeenth Century

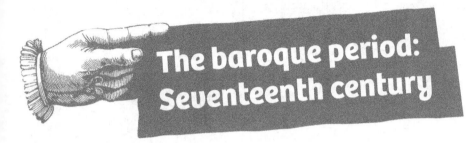

The baroque period: Seventeenth century

At the beginning of the seventeenth century, the New Spanish society was made up of indigenous people, Europeans, blacks who were brought as slaves, and some Chinese and Filipinos who emigrated when the *Nao de China* (China Ships) began.

Almost a century after the conquest, New Spain began to consolidate its identity. Miscegenation was encouraged by the decline in population of the indigenous people, who almost disappeared due to epidemics. Around 1700, with three generations of New Span-

ish born after the conquest, a different social dynamic was already apparent, with its own culture and gastronomy. The seventeenth century marked the beginning of the baroque period, which determined art and culture for more than a century.

During this century, Mexico City faced floods, plagues, cold waves, tremors, droughts, eclipses, and the sighting of comets, which frightened the people. It was a century of treachery, superstition, and fear, and enlightenment was slow in coming.

It was the time when legends were born, such as La Llorona, who cried out for her dead children; the legend of the Mulata of Córdoba, who escaped from the Inquisition in a boat she painted in the Perpetua prison; or that of Don Juan Manuel, a character who made the phrase "blessed are you who know the time of your death" famous.

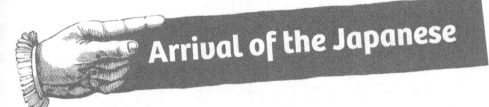

Arrival of the Japanese

On November 13, 1610, the New Spanish saw Japanese for the first time. They sailed as a commercial envoy with Europe as their destination. Japan was already known from the chronicles of travelers, but above all because of the martyrdom of a group of Jesuits, among them Philip of Jesus, in Nagasaki in 1597.

The Japanese envoy, headed by the shogun Tokuga-wa Ieyasu, arrived in Mexico City on December 16, 1610, and caused great excitement. The reception was impressive; people could not help but be amazed by their physical appearance, strange clothing, and the weapons they carried.

The most important and extensive description of the Japanese presence in New Spain was written by the Indian chronicler Chimalpahin, who at age thirty-one wrote in his diary:

> They all arrived dressed as they dress there: with a kind of [long] vest and a girdle at the waist, where they kept their steel katana, which is like a sword, and a mantilla. The sandals they wore were made of a finely tanned leather called chamois, like gloves for the feet. They were not shy, they were not gentle or humble, but looked like eagles [fierce].

The highlight of the visit was the conversion of two members of the envoy to the Christian faith. The church of Saint Francis was decorated on Sunday, January 23, 1611, for their baptism.

Flooding

The Spanish never liked the big lake that surrounded Mexico City because they considered it a constant threat. From the beginning of the seventeenth century, the viceregal authorities began the largest and most important, costly, and time-consuming public work in the country's history: the drainage of the Valley of Mexico. The goal was simple: to drain the lake. The task transcended dynasties, viceroys, presidents, governments, and everything before or after, and was finally concluded during the government of Porfirio Díaz.

The worst flood in Mexico's history occurred in September 1629, when it rained for thirty-six hours straight. The lake overflowed, and the capital of New

Spain was almost completely submerged. Only a small part of Tlatelolco and of the main square were spared. The small island that formed between the Viceroy's Palace and the cathedral was known as the Island of the Dogs, due to the large number of dogs that took refuge there.

The flood caused the deaths of more than thirty thousand people and forced twenty thousand families to evacuate the city. As the days went by, the people who remained in the capital went to the rooftops and balconies to listen to mass, which was also celebrated from the tops of buildings.

The Spanish crown ordered the city to be abandoned and rebuilt on the mainland, but the viceregal authorities argued against it. Five years later, when the waters had subsided, the capital of New Spain had only four hundred families. In spite of everything, the city did not change its location.

Justice

During the seventeenth century, legal issues were part and parcel of the daily lives of Mexico City's inhabitants. Everything was known; any piece of news, rumor, or gossip traveled the capital of New Spain. One of the most talked-about scandals occurred in the middle of the century.

At the beginning of the 1640s, Irish adventurer William Lamport, a great swordsman, pirate, intellectual, and revolutionary, appeared in the capital. He introduced himself to the viceroy as the natural son of King Philip III, which allowed him to get into the viceregal court.

Lamport's intentions were to liberate the indigenous nobility, free the slaves, and gain independence for New Spain. He was discovered and ended up in the hands of the Inquisition, which, in addition to the charge of sedition, accused him of sorcery and witchcraft and of having dealings with the Devil.

On Christmas Eve in 1650, after eight years of captivity, Lamport escaped from the Perpetua prison but was recaptured a few days later. On November 18, 1659, he was executed by the Inquisition in the Alameda Central.

Colonial justice was distinctive. It sought to be severe and strict in the application of the law and did not allow anyone, alive or dead, to make a mockery of it.

On March 7, 1649, a Portuguese man, awaiting the death penalty for the assassination of the sheriff of Iztapalapa, took his own life rather than suffer death at the hands of the executioner in the pillory on Plaza Mayor.

Upon discovering the corpse, the administrators of the court jail felt aggrieved. Suicide was a mockery of justice; he had to die, but not by his own hand. It was irrelevant that he was already dead, and they hanged the deceased man in the main square.

The palace in ruins

The worst social crisis Mexico City's viceregal government faced occurred in 1692. In recent years there had been severe droughts, and as a result, food was scarce and distributors profiteered from the situation. Uncharacteristically in the history of New Spain, the people rioted in front of the palace, demanding food and blaming the viceroy, Count of Galvéz, for the serious situation.

The angry mob looted the shops of Plaza Mayor, owned by Spaniards; stoned the Viceregal Palace; and looted warehouses and set them on fire.

The authorities regained control with the shedding of blood, put down the uprising with firepower, and hanged the leaders of the riot. Their bodies were displayed in the main square as a lesson. The palace viceroyalty had to be rebuilt.

The rebellion of 1692 became known as the "bread riot" because of the shortage of corn and wheat.

Culture and art

Although the baroque period in Europe began shortly before the end of the sixteenth century, it took time to reach New Spain and become established in the mid-seventeenth century. It was a slow but fruitful process, allowing local development of the arts with the creation of workshops, schools, and academies that promoted their own baroque style with artists of New Spanish origin.

Religion inspired the fine arts. Distinctive works reflected the exaltation of life, and religion and faith were depicted as part of daily life. The baroque was an ornate, decorative style, full of movement and form that was visible on façades, altarpieces, and chapels.

Although the great architectural accomplishments of the New Spanish baroque were created in the first half of the eighteenth century—like Jerónimo de Balbás's 1736 Altar of the Kings, the Cathedral of Mexico, and the 1750s church of Santa Prisca de Taxco—from the seventeenth century on, the New Spanish baroque revealed its splendor in the Virgin of the Rosary chapel, in the temple of Santo Domingo in the town of Puebla. It took forty years to build, from 1650 to 1690, and was considered the eighth wonder of the world.

One of the greatest painters of the period was Cristóbal de Villalpando, born in 1649 in Mexico City. A genius

and luminary of his time, he was a member of the painters' guild between 1686 and 1699.

Many of his works are in the Cathedral of Mexico City, such as *The Apotheosis of Saint Michael* and *Woman of the Apocalypse*, but without a doubt his masterpiece is *View of the Plaza Mayor*, made at the end of the seventeenth century, in which it is possible to admire daily life—the street trade, the market, and even the Viceroy's Palace, destroyed after the riot of 1692.

Other artists who left their mark were José Juárez, who based his work on engravings by Rubens that arrived in New Spain and whose best-known painting is *The Adoration of the Kings*; and Oaxacan Miguel Cabrera, who specialized in Marian themes, particularly the Virgin of Guadalupe. He painted the famous portrait of Sor Juana Inés de la Cruz around 1750.

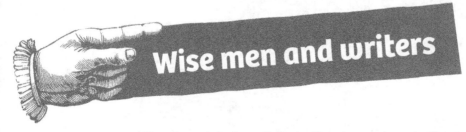

Wise men and writers

The playwright Juan Ruiz de Alarcón was born in Taxco, possibly around 1580. A physical defect earned him the ridicule of his contemporaries; he was a hunchback, but his natural talent for letters won him the recognition of the Spanish court. The history of Mexican literature proper begins with him.

He was a lawyer who lived a good part of his youth in New Spain but settled in Madrid in 1614. There he devoted himself to his profession as interim rapporteur of the Council of the Indies but was mainly given free rein to pursue his vocation as a playwright.

He began to receive honors and recognition from 1617 onward—no small feat, considering that he was a New Spaniard who had managed to gain a place in Madrid's political and literary circles. His plays, *The Favors of the World*, *The Walls Have Ears*, *Win Friends*, *The Cave of Salamanca*, *The Privileged Breasts*, and *Examination for Husbands*, were performed at the Royal Palace.

His works were collected and published between 1628 and 1634 as proof that they were his, since it was not uncommon for works to be attributed to other authors—as was the case with *The Suspicious Truth*, which was for some time believed to have been written by Félix Lope de Vega. Alarcón died in Madrid in 1639.

Carlos de Sigüenza y Góngora was a wise and erudite scholar, devoting himself to science, history, and geography. He was a mathematician, poet, writer, cosmographer, and professor of philosophy and exact sciences at the University of Mexico. Born in 1645 in Mexico City, he entered the Jesuit order at the age of fifteen.

Curiosity defined Góngora's personality, and he participated in scientific and colonizing expeditions. He oversaw the first archaeological excavations carried out in New Spain at Teotihuacan. He wrote almanacs, books on astronomy, and one for the good ruler: *Theater of Political Virtues*.

When the Viceroy's Palace was set on fire during the riot of 1692, Góngora paid a group of mutineers to help him rescue archives and works of art from the flames. For this action he received the appointment of Honorary Geographer by Appointment to His Majesty.

Another gifted mind of the seventeenth century was Juana Inés de Asbaje y Ramírez de Santillana, sometimes called the "phoenix of America" or the "tenth muse." Sor Juana was born in 1651 in Nepantla, in what is now the State of Mexico. Wise and erudite, she was the great poet of Mexican history. Her intelligence was so remarkable that at age seventeen she was subjected to a public examination in front of forty wise men, in which she was questioned on issues with the intention of determining whether her wisdom was "human or divine."

Juana joined the court of viceroy Antonio Sebastián Álvarez of Toledo, whose wife, Leonora, was her patron, protector, and friend. In 1669 she entered the convent of Saint Geronimo and took the name Sor Juana Inés de la Cruz. She was an accountant and archivist and began to interact with the viceroys and renowned figures of New Spain.

She composed the allegorical poem "Neptune," the verses of which were written on the great triumphal arch that received Viceroy Marquis de la Laguna in Mexico City in 1680. The poem enunciated maxims of wisdom and good government and were received with pleasure by the viceroy and his wife, the Countess of Paredes, who immediately became her protectors. By way of thanks, Sor Juana dedicated her book *Inundación castálida* to the countess, which made her famous in Mexico and in Spain. The poet found in the countess a great friend and dedicated several poems to her. In her poetic outpourings, Sor Juana called her "Divine Lysi."

Of all her poems, "First Dream," published in 1692 in the first volume of her complete works, was the most important.

According to her testimony, it was the only work that she wrote for pleasure.

Sor Juana was interested in astronomy, mathematics, philosophy, mythology, history, music, and painting. This was frowned upon in a seventeenth-century woman, but her talent prevailed over prejudice. In 1693 she abandoned her writing, got rid of her personal library and her musical and scientific instruments, and gave her money to the poor. She died in 1695. Five years later, her contemporary Carlos de Sigüenza y Góngora died.

My divine Lysi:
do forgive my daring,
if I address you so,
unworthy though I am to be
known as yours.

I cannot think it bold
to call you so, well knowing
you've ample thunderbolts
to shatter any overweening
of mine.

...

Thus, when I call you
mine, it's not that I expect
you'll be considered such
only that I hope I may
be yours.

The
Eighteenth Century

Nothing to the imagination

The end of the seventeenth century coincided with the end of the Habsburg dynasty, which had dominated Spanish possession of the Americas since the sixteenth century. Left behind were two centuries of history.

The new century would bring great changes for New Spain and, in particular, for the royals and faithful of Mexico City.

The capital's inhabitants were speechless when, in 1702, they saw the arrival of the new viceroy, Francisco Fernández, Duke of Albuquerque, dressed outrageously in two-inch red heels, ruffled bowtie, long powdered Louis XIV–style wig, velvet coat, silk pants, and white stockings.

But if the viceroy attracted attention, his wife stole the show, with a plunging neckline that left nothing to the imagination and a fitted dress embroidered with gold and silver thread, rhinestones, sequins, and beads.

The fashion was an announcement of the times that were about to begin and reflected the change in the reigning dynasty; the Habsburg period had ended, giving way to the era of the Bourbons.

For more than 150 years, New Spain had been accustomed to the austere and conservative fashion of the Austrian house, which consisted of the use of black-and-white clothing for all occasions, for both men and women, and dresses up to the neck.

Daily life was filled with garish colors, lace, silk, and jewels of all kinds that accompanied ladies' necklines. Even the habit of smoking tobacco was abandoned in exchange for inhaling it; it was the age of snuffboxes. The eighteenth century had begun.

Capital news and novelties

The eighteenth century brought many novelties to the daily life of New Spain. Between 1710 and 1716, during the government of the Duke of Linares, the viceroy at the time, Mexico's first public library was dedicated, the first animal and plant museum in the Americas opened, and the first opera companies arrived and performed at the Viceroy's Palace. Admission was free to every stratum of society, even though no one was very interested in listening to opera.

In 1722 King Felipe V announced the need to "pursue criminals and thugs who had infested the kingdom," and the Agreement Tribunal was established. Its jail was built near the Alameda Central, presently the corner of Juárez and Bucareli streets, and was notorious for its punishments and for the screams of prisoners locked up in the dungeons.

The viceroy, Marquis of Casa Fuerte, who governed from 1722 to 1734, was repudiated for prohibiting the celebrations of the Mexico City carnival, which heralded the beginning of Lent, although he allowed them at Ixtacalco. To escape the festivities' hustle and bustle, he also ordered construction of the Paseo de la Viga.

New Spain's first newspaper, the *Mexican Gazette and News from New Spain*, began circulating in Mexico City in January 1722. It was eight pages long and, for various reasons, lasted just six months. In 1728 a new gazette was published although it had been in existence for eleven years; it only had four pages.

The *Mexico Gazette* covered notable events, celebrity obituaries, peace campaigns in the territory of New Spain, religious matters, history, science, natural phenomena, epidemics, earthquakes, and even comets. It was not a newspaper of political criticism but rather a detailed chronicle of what was most relevant for New Spain, in the opinion of its editor.

Issue 6 of the *Mexico Gazette* changed its name to *A Historical Anthology of Mexico and News of New Spain*.

The city's first theater, the Coliseum, was built in 1673 in the Royal Hospital. It was destroyed by fire in 1722, and in 1753 a new Coliseum opened on present-day Calle Bolívar. The center of theatrical activity until 1820, it eventually became known as the Teatro Principal and existed until 1931, when another fire put an end to its history.

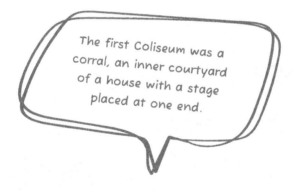

The first Coliseum was a corral, an inner courtyard of a house with a stage placed at one end.

Another event that marked the eighteenth century, one that continues in Mexico to this day, is the lottery. The first draw was held on May 13, 1771, and the first prize was ten thousand pesos. Since then there have been "screamers" who move the machines with the numbers and announce them by shouting.

It was the century of institutions: in 1781 the Royal Academy of San Carlos was created, where painting, sculpture, and architecture were taught; the first Natural History Museum was created in 1790; and at the end of the century what we know today as the General Archive of the Nation was also created.

Honoring the dead

If there was one thing the capital of New Spain did not lack, it was cemeteries. They were as numerous and as varied as the churches that stood over the entire Valley of Mexico. In 1736 alone, when smallpox ravaged the region, there were more than twenty-five.

It was common for ecclesiastical authorities and monastic orders to use church atria and hospital interiors to carry out burials. Next to each religious building was an area of land for a cemetery.

There seemed to be an inconspicuous competition to offer places in the afterlife, the destination of all the invocations to the Virgin Mary and the saints who gave their names to religious buildings: Saint Michael, Saint Catherine, Santa Veracruz, Saint Santiago Tlatelolco, Saint Dominic, and Our Lady of Mercy, among others. In the three centuries of Spanish domination, there were never as many cemeteries registered as in 1736. One of the most famous was the pantheon of Saint Paula, which opened its doors to the deceased in 1779 when smallpox returned to claim many of the poorest victims.

The Hospital of Saint Andrew, on Calle Tacuba, owned the cemetery and, faced with this health crisis, arranged a place for patients who did not respond to medical treatment and whose only alternative was to surrender to death.

The cemetery was constructed on the city's outskirts, in what today is part of north Paseo de la Reforma, in front of the building that for years was occupied by the Mexico Tent Theater. For years, only the sick who died in Saint Andrew Hospital were buried there.

The chapel bell of Saint Paula cemetery announced to the vicar the entrance of the deceased, whose funerals he performed and whose graves he blessed. Burials took place at night to protect the city from witnessing the sad funeral processions.

The years passed, and Saint Paula, like the country, changed when Mexico achieved independence. In 1836 it was declared a general cemetery, and anyone who died in Mexico City could be buried there. It was said to be "the best cemetery in the whole Republic ...it knew how to unite mournful beauty with healthiness, decency, and cleanliness."

Saint Paula also received the mortal remains of men and women who gave their lives for the Mexican cause, such as the insurgent Leona Vicario and several of the patriots who fought against the Amer-

icans in the battles of King's Mill and Chapultepec Castle in September 1847, among them Lucas Balderas and Felipe Santiago Xicoténcatl. It also made history when Antonio López de Santa Anna organized a funeral in 1842 for his leg, which he lost when he was hit by a grenade in 1839 during the Pastry War.

By 1869 Mexico City's government had ordered the cemetery's closure to make room for new ones. With the city's growth, the construction and roads erased the last vestiges of Saint Paula and most of its inhabitants.

The ill-fated castle

During three centuries of Spanish domination, Chapultepec forest was always considered a place "on the outskirts of the city" and remained so at the end of the nineteenth century. It had been established by royal decree in 1530 that the entire forest would be the property of Mexico City in perpetuity for the recreation and relaxation of its inhabitants.

During the eighteenth century, buildings began to appear in the forest, including the King's Mill, where wheat and corn were ground; a hilltop gunpowder

factory established in 1764 that burned down on four occasions before finally exploding on November 19, 1784; and Chapultepec Castle.

In the seventeenth century's first decade, the viceroy, Duke of Albuquerque, ordered construction of a summer residence on the remains of what had been the Palace of Nezahualcoyotl. It was a country mansion that included a bullfighting ring.

For decades the estate was the venue for lavish parties organized to welcome the viceroy, until the Spanish crown prohibited them in 1739 because of their profligacy and the debauchery guests surrendered to beside the centuries-old cypresses. In addition, the distance from Mexico City became a problem, as Chapultepec was too far from the capital and maintenance of the residence too costly. Thus the residence fell into disrepair.

In 1784 the viceroy, Don Matías de Gálvez, took an interest in Chapultepec and ordered construction of a fortress. But death surprised him. His son, Bernardo de Gálvez, was the successor, and beginning in 1785 he supervised the magnum opus that was built at unprecedented speed.

It didn't take long for gossips to appear, and rumors spread like wildfire. For many it was suspicious that the construction was not a summer residence but a fortified castle; that it was financed, for the most part, with public resources but also with funds from the viceroy himself; that the works were directed by the military; and that hundreds of men, including numerous convicts, worked day and night to finish.

Viceroy Gálvez had the admiration of the people, but he behaved like the sovereign, not as his representative, and this disturbed the court. Several of its members wrote to Spain warning that the viceroy would make New Spain independent and proclaim himself ruler of the Chapultepec fortress.

These accusations were never proven. It is not even known if the viceroy's intention was to assume absolute power; Don Bernardo took his secrets to the grave, dying in 1787. It is believed that he was poisoned.

The unfinished work was soon abandoned again and remained so until the 1830s. By then Mexico was independent, and the castle was an unenviable shell; the best things about the property were the forest, cypresses, pools, and fountains that surrounded it.

On November 16, 1833, President Santa Anna issued a decree creating the Military College, stipulating that it should be housed in the "palace, forest, and fabric" of Chapultepec. It was not until 1841, however, that the castle was in condition to receive cadets at the college, which began offering courses in 1842.

"With complete freedom," chronicler Francisco Sedano wrote in News of México, "at any hour of the day, they throw into the streets, filthy vessels, garbage, manure, and dead dogs . . . Anyone, without respect for public decency, would litter the streets or wherever."

The great modernization

When Viceroy Don Juan Vicente Güemes Pacheco de Padilla, Count of Revillagigedo, arrived in Mexico City in 1789, the capital was a mess. People tossed their garbage in the streets or threw their urine from the windows, hence the cry "*aguas*" (water), warning passersby to watch out when passing.

Itinerant and permanent trade in the Parián, the large market operating in the Plaza Mayor since the end of the seventeenth century, left the square looking like a dunghill, and a fetid odor permeated the air. The once-transparent water ditches had turned into rivulets of sewage.

The Viceroy's Palace was a reflection of the pestilential city:

> "Inside," Francisco Sedano wrote, "were living quarters and stallholders in the plaza, warehouses of fruit and groceries, an inn and a wine shop called the Botillería, a bakery, diners where pulque was sold publicly, a secret bar, public gambling, a bowling alley, and rubbish dumps."

Late-night revelers considered the palace to be the place to continue the party. Flamboyant people, thugs, beggars, and belligerent drunks gave an even more somber aspect to the seat of New Spanish power. The place where Moctezuma's splendid palace once stood was an expanse of decay and filth left daily by vendors in the Plaza Mayor. As if that were not enough, there was nothing worse than seeing people urinating and defecating in public.

Aware of the need for a public health policy, the viceroy issued a decree in August 1790 to clean up Mexico City, and like any visionary, he went further: he considered the problem to also be one of education, which is why he decided schools should teach students to practice good hygiene:

> Schoolteachers must take special care to ensure that children are brought up with due modesty and decorum. They will see to it that they are clean and tidy, having places in schools intended for this purpose, where they will be allowed to go one by one, under the irrevocable penalty of deprivation of exercise from the teacher for anyone who fails at something so essential to good education.

Thus began the viceroy's great crusade to modernize and clean up the city. He introduced gutters and drainage, paved the streets, established a cleaning and garbage collection service, put a number on each house, and installed public lighting with oil lamps.

In addition, he ordered the beautification of the promenades and avenues, controlled the city's traffic chaos, and introduced the first rental cars to the capital.

On August 15, 1793, the viceroy authorized the use of cars for public service. Initially there were only eight carriages. They had to be closed, numbered, and colored green and yellow. They could only be boarded at Saint Dominic's Square, the Merchants' Gate in front of the Viceroy's Palace, or on Calle del Arzobispado.

The cars operated from seven in the morning to nine at night. At the end of a trip, it was the driver's responsibility to remind passengers to remember their belongings. The drivers had to be polite and decent, wear a uniform, and "be mindful that not even for the greatest urgency must they run or gallop within the city." These carriages were the first taxis in Mexico.

The viceroy also created the police service, called *serenos* (night watchmen), to serve both day and night. He mercilessly pursued thieves and murderers, and his government's iron fist fell upon the criminals. Thanks to Revillagigedo, the capital of New Spain was known as the City of Palaces.

The night watchman of the city was immortalized in these song lyrics: "Would the night watchman on the corner do me the favor of turning off his flashlight, as my love passes by."

Near the turn of the century, the capital welcomed one of its most emblematic monuments. With the pretext that New Spanish society madly loved their king, Charles IV, in 1796 the viceroy, Marquis de Branciforte, requested authorization to place an equestrian statue of the king in the Plaza Mayor.

Renowned architect and sculptor Manuel Tolsá worked on the statue for seven years. On November 17, 1803, the sculpture was ready; it took five days to make the 1,253-meter trip from the foundry to the square.

On December 9, 1803, the statue was finally unveiled; it remained in the square until the consummation of independence. The day the Army of the Three Guarantees (Trigarante) entered Mexico City, authorities covered the statue. Irrespective of its beauty, Charles IV no longer held a place in an independent Mexico. Days later it was moved to the University of Mexico courtyard.

In 1852 authorities decided to install the statue at the entrance of Bucareli. On a whim of President Mariano Arista, it was placed so it was visible from the National Palace. The operation began on September 11 and concluded on September 25.

The statue remained there until 1979, when it rode for the last time to Avenida Tacuba, in front of the Palace of Communications (now the National Museum of Art) and the Palace of Mining, in so-called Plaza Tolsá, where it stands today.

The streets of the historic center

In colonial Mexico, the only two streets that ran westward from Plaza Mayor were Tacuba and present-day Madero. The latter, which was always the principal street, is known as Saint Francis and the Silversmiths.

The first section of the famous street took its name from one of the most impressive convents in Hispanic America: San Francisco el Grande. This section of Plateros was home to New Spain's most important jewelers, whose gold and silver pieces were true works of art.

It was an important street in terms of buildings. It began in San Juan de Letrán with the Guardiola Garden and the House of Ceramics, where the famous Jockey Club was established. A little farther on, in the direction of the Zócalo, were the temple of San Felipe Neri and the monumental Iturbide Palace. Another famous church that rang its bells on that street was La Profesa. A few meters away from Plaza Mayor, dozens of jewelry stores were on display for the curious. With the Mexican Revolution, the street acquired a new name.

Pancho Villa's devotion to Francisco I. Madero was so great that in December 1914 he renamed the entire avenue to honor the apostle of democracy. Since then, it has been called Francisco I. Madero. To ensure that no one tried to change the name, Villa issued a threat to the world, swearing to destroy anyone who dared remove the name of "his" lay saint from the street. More than a hundred years later, its corner still reads "Ave. Fco. I Madero."

The Jockey Club was the meeting place for the upper class during the administration of Porfirio Díaz. Among its members were José Limantour, Pablo Escandón Barrón, Guillermo Landa Escandón, and Ignacio Torres Adalid.

In previous times, Avenida 16 de Septiembre had been a waterway, navigable only by canoe. The palace acequia, one of the city's seven great irrigation ditches, ran along its route, and for this reason it continued to be known as Calle la Acequia in the seventeenth century and the first half of the eighteenth. Around 1790 the acequia was emptied and converted into a dirt road with the following names: El Refugio, after a statue of the Virgin was placed there to provide divine intervention protecting parishioners from crime; the Old Coliseum; and Tlapaleros (the tinkerers), the last part of the street before one entered the Zócalo at one of its corners.

In 1856, when a confrontation between Liberals and Conservatives loomed on the horizon, a conspiracy against the Liberal government of Ignacio Comonfort was discovered on the eve of Independence Day. The punishment was to demolish part of the Congress to open a street that was subsequently renamed Independence.

Avenida 16 de Septiembre was home to the oldest theater in New Spain, which burned down in 1722. It was where the Great Society Hotel, the Fruit Gate of the late seventeenth century, and many other portals and colonial houses renovated in the nineteenth century were located. In the nineteenth century the street acquired the name it bears today, which commemorates the beginning of the War of Independence—Avenida 16 de Septiembre.

At the beginning of the nineteenth century, carriages avoided Calle Alcaicería, which adjoins the house of La Profesa. The old street was so short and narrow that José Marroquí, in his book *Mexico City*, called it "a sad, ugly alley." But urbanization would not be slow in coming to this forgotten street.

In 1861, after several improvement plans, the decision was made to extend the street west up to Vergara (today Calle Bolívar). To achieve this goal, engineers faced the challenge of demolishing some houses and part of the house of La Profesa and the Santa Clara convent.

Work began in February of that year. Within a few months, the house of La Profesa had been divided, and in the middle a beautiful wide street began to form. But its barely nascent beauty did not spark people's interest to inhabit it. The Santa Clara convent was in ruins, and the almost chaste cells could be seen from the street. Respect for the building, which had been a victim of reform laws, meant that the new avenue remained abandoned for some time.

After the heroic battle of Puebla, on May 5, 1862, where the Mexicans defeated the first army in the world, the street was baptized with the date of the glorious event. "I promise you a day of glory," Gen. Ignacio Zaragoza said, hours before the battle. He delivered. In one of the corners, near the church of La Profesa (the Church of San Felipe Neri), a plaque was placed explaining the street name, 5 de Mayo. It didn't last long; the French occupied Mexico City in June 1863. Realizing that the avenue had been named for the day its army was defeated, some members of the invading troops drew their pistols and fired at the plaque until it was destroyed. In spite of everything, for the capital's inhabitants it was still 5 de Mayo.

With the Republic's triumph and the defeat of the French and Maximilian's empire (1867), the street's expansion continued. But its moment of splendor came in 1881. By then, 5 de Mayo was more than had been planned twenty years earlier. It started on Calle del Empedradillo (cobblestone street, today Monte de Piedad), which overlooked the Zócalo, and ended on Vergara (today Calle Bolívar) in front of the Teatro Principal, which gave its last performance in 1900 with the opera *Aida*. A year later the old building was demolished to extend the street farther, reaching San Juan de Letran (today Eje Central), in front of the theater that was built in 1904 next to the Alameda Central.

The present-day street of Allende, along with its continuation Bolívar, crosses Donceles, Tacuba, 5 de Mayo, Madero, 16 de Septiembre, and several other streets before reaching José María Izazaga. As was the custom in colonial times, the names referred to some trade or place in each section—Calle del Factor, Vergara, and Coliseo Nuevo—but in reality the entire street was defined by the fact that the city's main theaters were located along it. From north to south, on the corner of Factor and Donceles, stood the Iturbide Theater, which in 1872 housed the Chamber of Deputies because its premises in the National Palace had burned down.

Legislators found the place and its location comfortable and remained there until 1909, when the building was remodeled. It reopened in 1911 to receive the resignation of Porfirio Díaz; legislative sessions were held there until 1981, when the Chamber of Deputies was relocated to Saint Lazarus. This famous building is now occupied by the Congress of Mexico City.

The Great Theater of Santa Anna, dubbed the Imperial Theater in the time of Maximilian, was always known as the National Theater. Construction began in 1842, and its doors opened in 1844. After more than half a century of fame, it was demolished in 1900 for two reasons: to extend Avenida 5 de Mayo and because Porfirio Díaz's government wanted to build a new national theater, known today as Bellas Artes.

The third theater on this long street was the Coliseo Nuevo, dedicated in 1752 and renamed the Teatro Principal once Mexico achieved independence. At the beginning of the twentieth century it became well known for its pantomime and revue shows, but in the 1930s it caught fire, and that's where its story ends.

Avenida Juárez is the prelude to Avenida Madero, beginning at the spot where the El Caballito (little horse) statue had been, and where Bucareli also started. The first section, heading toward Plaza Mayor, was known as Calle del Calvario after an eighteenth-century chapel where the Stations of the Cross ended and the temple of San Francisco began.

The next section was formed by Calle Acordada, where the building of the same name stood; during the colonial period it served as a prison. Hospice for the Poor and Corpus Christi Streets formed the avenue's final section, which led to the Guardiola Garden and the House of Tiles. This was where the Alameda, Mexico's most traditional promenade, was located; in front was the Convent of Corpus Christi, which was occupied by Capuchin Indian nuns. Around 1925 the temple fell into the hands of the schismatic church of the patriarch José Joaquín Pérez Budar, who tried to create a Mexican Catholic church independent of Rome.

The avenue took its name from a historical fact. On July 15, 1867, Benito Juárez returned victorious to Mexico City after a four-year pilgrimage around the country defending the legality of his investiture as president of the Republic against Maximilian's empire. The city organized a grand reception, and the president made his triumphal entry through the old streets that told a history and that since then have collectively been known as Juárez Avenue.

Capital of the Republic

For almost three centuries, the largest viceroyalty in the Americas had weathered tremors, floods, epidemics, riots, and political and economic reforms that threatened the most precious jewel in the Spanish crown. They put the legendary capital city at risk and shook even the last column of the Viceroy's Palace. But the adversities also cemented its strength. The year 1800 heralded the arrival of the nineteenth century and showed New Spain to be more solid than at any other time since 1521.

Mexico City looked splendid. Commerce developed within the Parián, a stone building on the square's south side; the fountain maintained its crystal-clear waters; and the pillory was a symbol of authority, then held by Viceroy José de Iturrigaray. To one side of the palace stood Plaza del Volador, where street trade was based, and in front, on the south side of Plaza Mayor, was the town hall.

Daily life seemed suspended in time; it was still marked by the bells of the cathedral and other temples in the city signaling prayer times. Religious holidays such as Easter, Christmas, the celebration of the Virgin of Guadalupe, the Day of the Dead, and civic holidays such as Paseo del Pendón on August 13, which recalled the Spanish triumph over the Mexica empire, were part of the fabric of the city.

The capital of New Spain looked like the best example of the future. By 1805, the city had almost 150,000 inhabitants and 304 streets, 140 alleys, 12 bridges, 64 squares, 21 inns, and 28 corrals. About 30 taxis circulated through the town, and from that year on it could boast of having the first daily publication in Mexican history: *El Diario de México*.

Daily commerce, public and ecclesiastical affairs, as well as professions, devotions, and most entertainment took place in what is now known as the historic center, although the most distant promenades, still within the city, were the Alameda and Bucareli. During religious holidays, it was common for people of all classes to go to Chapultepec forest or even farther, to the towns of Tacubaya, San Agustín de las Cuevas (Tlalpan), Coyoacán, Santa Anita, or Ixtacalco.

Times of change

The year 1800 brought many changes for a New Spanish society that believed it had seen everything. From the Atlantic came news from Europe, and from the Pacific Ocean—the Philippines, Japan, and China—came news, goods, and even animals.

Amazing as it may seem, until then no one in New Spain had ever seen a live elephant. That is why the arrival of a ship carrying a live elephant in the Port of Veracruz was the great event of 1800. The *Mexico Gazette* even announced it as an animal "never seen in these realms."

For 360 pesos, someone had acquired the impressive animal in Veracruz and saw a business opportunity. It was a ten-year-old female that had traveled much of the world. After being captured and trained in Asia, it went to the United States, then to Cuba, and finally to Mexico.

The promoter settled in the capital and, with the viceroy's authorization, opened his business at 5 Colorado Bridge Street on the corner of Callejón de la Danza. People could see the beauty and grace of the elephant for only two royals. Her tusks were not long, but they were long enough to show their greatness.

She was a sweet-toothed elephant, and the audience couldn't help but be moved by her enjoying cakes at the

convenient times from 8 a.m. to 1 p.m., and from 3 p.m. "until the time for prayers."

In those early years of the nineteenth century, nothing seemed to alter the order in New Spain, much less in Mexico City. The winds of liberation were blowing, however, and they turned into a storm in 1808 when Napoleon Bonaparte decided to invade Spain, depose King Charles IV and his successor, Ferdinand VII, and leave the throne to his brother Pepe Botella (bottle), as he was known because of his fondness for alcohol.

The creoles of the capital's city hall attempted a coup, declaring that as long as the crown was not in the hands of the legitimate king, the sovereignty returned to the people, who were represented by the members of the town hall. This first attempt at independence, however, was stifled by the Spaniards living in the capital.

The event shook the capital and ended with the assassination of Francisco Primo de Verdad, a city council member who was found dead in his cell in October 1808. From the moment the priest Miguel Hidalgo y Costilla and the insurgent army threatened to take Mexico City in 1811 (an event that did not materialize), the capital's inhabitants watched the war of independence from afar.

Hearing news of the campaign against the insurgents but living in tranquility until September 27, 1821, Agustín de Iturbide made his triumphal entry at the head of the Army of the Three Guarantees, signifying the consummation of independence. That day was the first time in history that Mexico City wore the three colors of the future flag: green, white, and red.

"The houses were adorned with arcs of flowers of a thousand whimsical forms in the Trigarante colors, which the women also wore on the ribbons and bows of their dresses in their hair," Lucas Alamán wrote. "The joy was universal. It can be said that September 27, 1821, has been the only day of pure enthusiasm and joy that Mexicans have enjoyed."

The Federal District

Although Mexico was born into independent life as an empire, the monarchy did not sit well with the new country, and in 1824 it adopted the republican form of government. With the new political division, Mexico City was in the State of Mexico, the largest entity in the country, which by then was so extensive that it equaled the area of the states of Morelos, Hidalgo, Guerrero, and parts of Tlaxcala and Querétaro, even bordering the Pacific Ocean on the south.

Since the natural capital of the State of Mexico was Mexico City, its first governor, Melchor Múzquiz, established his offices in the building that had been the seat of the Inquisition, in the Plaza of Santo Domingo, and the local representatives met next to the National Palace, in the present-day streets of Correo Mayor, the main post office.

Federal representatives quickly concluded that Mexico City could not be the capital of any state in the Republic, but rather an autonomous entity with the powers of federation. Thus, on November 18, 1824, the Federal District was created. It disappeared in 2017 when it became the thirty-second state republic, called Mexico City.

Overnight the State of Mexico was left without what had been the capital of New Spain, but Congress authorized that its governor and its local congress could remain in the Federal District in the exercise of their functions, while they chose the place to establish a capital for the State of Mexico.

As of February 1, 1827, Congress established the state capital in Texcoco "because of its location neither too distant nor too close to Mexico City" and because it had a brilliant historical past: the kings of Texcoco had vied for their wisdom and culture with the Mexica emperors.

Texcoco, however, was a town without sufficient infrastructure to hold state powers and lacked accessible communication routes to Mexico City. For a few weeks the legislature had to meet in the pews of a church, convent cells were used for the courts, and the treasury was established in a private house.

Despite these problems, Texcoco had the honor of being the State of Mexico's capital where the first local constitution was promulgated on February 14, 1827. The deputies swore to the Magna Carta by placing their right hand on the Gospels and raising a crucifix with their left hand to kiss it. The festivities lasted for three days, but the popular uproar did not prevent Congress from changing the state capital to the town of San Agustín de las Cuevas.

The powers of the State of Mexico arrived at their new capital in June 1827, and one of the first measures was to restore its original name, which before the arrival of the Spaniards had been Tlalpan.

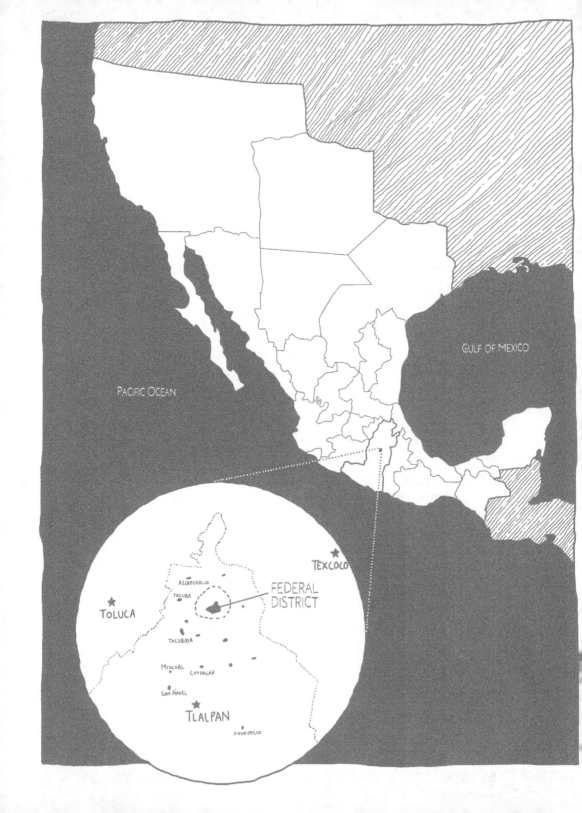

PACIFIC OCEAN

GULF OF MEXICO

TEXCOCO

TOLUCA

AZCAPOZALCO

TACUBA

FEDERAL
DISTRICT

TACUBAYA

MIXCOAC

COYOACÁN

SAN ÁNGEL

TLALPAN

XOCHIMILCO

As the State of Mexico's capital, Tlalpan developed rapidly. A palace was built with supreme powers, a mint, a cigar and cigarette factory, a gazette that published official proceedings, a literary institute, a first-class school of literature, a pharmacy, and a pre-Hispanic museum. The modest southern town became a thriving city with a promising future.

Tlalpan's proximity to Mexico City, however, was problematic both for the federal government and the State of Mexico's government. The national authority spent its time intervening in local affairs, revenues, and the legislature; exploiting its troops and resources; and, most seriously of all, diminishing the governor's authority. For its part, Tlalpan became the center of political conspiracy against the federal government. In order to avoid a definitive breakup, and in an attempt to allow the State of Mexico to initiate an autonomous and stable period of development, the local congress decided to change the state's capital for the last time and designated, as of 1830, the city of Toluca as the definitive seat. Over time Tlalpan became part of Mexico City.

Santa Anna's revolutions

In those first decades of independent life, Mexico City could well have been called Pronouncement City. Lucas Alamán called this period the "era of Santa Anna's revolutions." A large number of uprisings that started in Mexico City, or in other states in the country, ended up being headed by the Jalapeño general, who took the opportunity to lead any cause and make his grand entrance in the country's capital amid popular acclaim.

Around 1840 the Marchioness Calderón de la Barca, wife of the first Spanish ambassador, made an accurate account of all the armed movements that had taken place in Mexico since 1810 and said they could be predicted "like an eclipse of the sun":

All Mexicans under forty witnessed the revolution of Dolores in 1810, its continuation by Morelos . . . ; Iturbide's revolution in 1821; the Grito de Libertad (shout of liberty) given in 1822 by the generals, "worthies of the homeland," Santa Anna and Victoria; establishment of the federal system in 1824; the horrible revolution of the Acordada in 1828, in which Mexico City was sacked; the adoption of the central system in 1836; and the last revolution of the federalists in 1840.

Except for the 1828 mutiny of the Acordada, which ended with burning the Parián in the Plaza Mayor, Mexico City was generally respected by rival factions. Perhaps that is why the capital surrendered so easily to the victorious leader; after all, the citizens knew that whoever occupied the country's capital had the power.

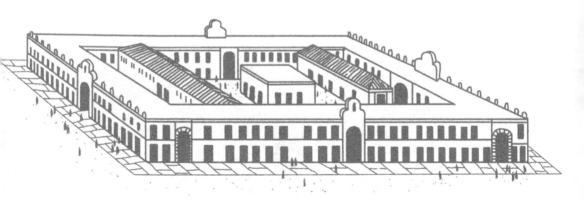

During the 1838 Pastry War, the leader who answered the call to arms to face the French lost a leg from shrapnel, which earned him the recognition of his fellow citizens. For some time, at least, Santa Anna managed to ascend to the altar of the homeland, and Mexico City acknowledged this by participating in his 1842 state funeral, organized to bury his leg in Saint Paula cemetery.

But the same crowd became angry with their leader. They exhumed his leg in 1844 and dragged it through Mexico City. They then pardoned him and cheered him again, later recognizing him as His Serene Highness, and finally dismissing him forever—all in seventeen years. Thus ended Santa Anna's romance with Mexico City.

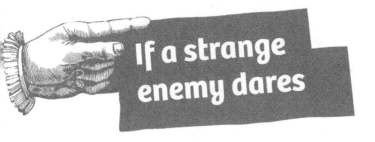

If a strange enemy dares

From 1847 to 1867, Mexico was radically transformed. After two years of war with the United States, in 1848 Mexico lost half its territory. Santa Anna disappeared from the political scene (1855). A new constitution (1857) was signed, which gave rise to the Reform War (1858–61) and a definitive confrontation between Liberals and Conservatives. The reform laws were passed (1859), and after several years the Republic triumphed over French intervention, and the second empire, with Maximilian, and the Conservatives disintegrated (1861–67). During those years foreign armies, thousands of Conservatives and Liberals, military men, presidents, and even a couple of emperors entered and left Mexico City.

The capital's inhabitants had to learn to coexist with invading U.S. troops from September 1847 to June 1848, during which time they remained an occupying army. By then most of the merchants were listing the names of their businesses in English and taking advantage of the fact that "gringos" paid with cash.

Mexico City was the first capital of a country the U.S. military occupied in its history.

The military occupation wasn't the only thing the capital suffered. On January 11, 1861, Benito Juárez made his triumphal entry into Mexico City after defeating the Conservatives in the Reform War. The reception was, according to chronicles of the time, "a true triumphal march."

But two years later he was forced to leave the capital because the French had the idea of invading Mexico, and in June 1863 they were received with applause. Conservative authorities even gave the keys to the city to Marshal Élie Frédéric Forey, general-in-chief of the occupying army.

A year later society again gave itself up with fascination and enthusiasm—and several triumphal arches—to Maximilian and Carlota, who entered the city on June 12, 1864. But the fascination didn't last long. After three years of resistance, Republicans defeated the empire and left Maximilian dead. On July 15, 1867, Don Benito returned victorious to Mexico City. The people of the capital, so as not to abandon the custom, gave the triumphant president a standing ovation. They were always with the winner.

Earthquakes

On June 19, 1858, a strong earthquake was felt in Mexico City. It was not the social earthquake of the Reform War between Liberals and Conservatives but rather nature taking a roll call of the country's capital.

Descriptions by foreign travelers and some Mexican writers concur that earthquakes were a common phenomenon in the city, one to which no one would ever become accustomed.

When they felt the earth move and heard the threatening creaking of the walls, people ran from their homes in search of squares and gardens, any place they felt would provide safety. Religious fervor flourished with greater intensity and the streets looked like huge prie-dieux, where the people of the capital implored the Creator's mercy.

Once the earth's fury had passed, only the name of the saint on whose day the earth had decided to chastise mankind remained in people's memories. This is how the most important ones were identified: the earthquake of San Juan de Dios (Saint John of God), of the Incarnation, and of Santa Mónica.

At that time, around 1840, I was deeply impressed by the earthquake of Saint Cecilia, which occurred at midnight: people left their beds half-naked and confessed their sins in the middle of the streets; priests beat their faces against the earth and raised their hands to the sky; the towers swayed, the bells rang like aching joints, and the fountains poured out their waters in terror.

— Guillermo Prieto

The people maintained that Mexico City's high temperatures in the spring made it the season for earthquakes. The earthquake of San Epifanio, on April 7, 1845, caused the most damage. One eyewitness at the time wrote:

> Shortly before the stroke of four in the afternoon, the most horrible tremor ever seen was felt. It lasted only a few minutes; the force of the shaking was terrible. No one remembers another like it, and the state of the buildings indicated that nature had never rocked the city's foundations so strongly.

In order to reassure the people, J. G. Cortina's newspaper article, "Earthquakes," listed only those earthquakes that had occurred since the conquest of Mexico. According to Cortina's research, seventy-three were recorded in the sixteenth century; sixty-nine in the seventeenth; twenty-four in the eighteenth; and at least six at the time of the article's publication in the nineteenth. He warned the population not to be scared anymore, since the city's buildings and structures were solid enough to withstand any earthquake; the ones that had been damaged owed their destruction to their owners' negligence and abandonment. His conclusion, however, was somewhat simplistic:

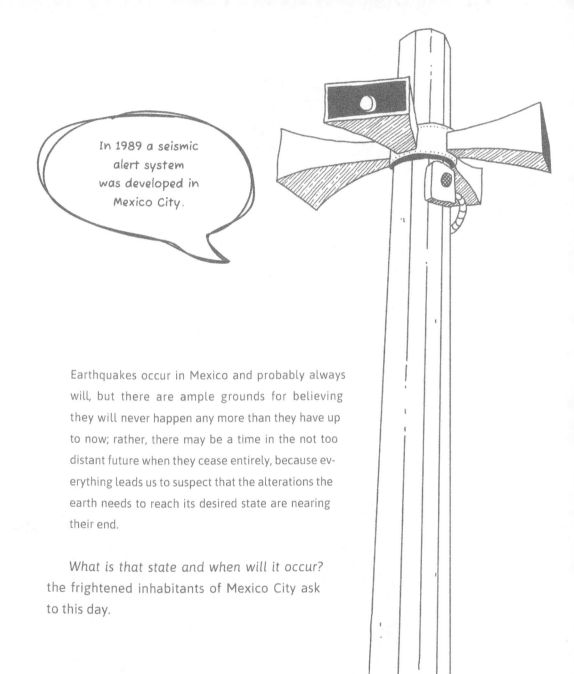

In 1989 a seismic alert system was developed in Mexico City.

Earthquakes occur in Mexico and probably always will, but there are ample grounds for believing they will never happen any more than they have up to now; rather, there may be a time in the not too distant future when they cease entirely, because everything leads us to suspect that the alterations the earth needs to reach its desired state are nearing their end.

What is that state and when will it occur? the frightened inhabitants of Mexico City ask to this day.

Epidemic

During the nineteenth century, not only did Mexico City's inhabitants have to learn to cope with armed uprisings, military occupations, and earthquakes; they also had to deal with two terrible epidemics of cholera morbus, in 1833 and 1850.

In 1833 Vice President Valentín Gómez Farías, who held power while President Santa Anna relaxed at his hacienda in Manga de Clavo, decided to push for reforms to put an end to the privileges of the clergy and the army; in simple terms, he tried to separate the Church from the State.

That year had been particularly hot; unhealthy conditions in the cities and, above all, in the capital, led to stagnation of sewage and contamination of water and foodstuffs. Cholera morbus spread uncontrollably, and the number of victims was sadly reminiscent of the epidemics that decimated the indigenous population in the sixteenth and seventeenth centuries.

The Church found in the epidemic its best weapon in combating Gómez Farías's liberal reforms and stirred up the population against the government. The Church did not deny holy oils nor medical assistance, much less worship, but it spread the rumor that the epidemic was divine punishment for government policy.

In Mexico City, where it is estimated that more than nineteen thousand died, scenes were apocalyptic. Guillermo Prieto wrote:

The silent and deserted streets in which the hurried footsteps of someone running for help echoed in the distance; the yellow, black, and white banners that served to warn of the disease, of doctors, priests, and houses of charity; the apothecary shops crowded with people; the temples with their doors wide open and a thousand lights on the altars, the people kneeling with folded arms, shedding tears. . . . In the distance, the lugubrious creak of hearses passing through the streets, the cemeteries of Santiago Tlatelolco, San Lázaro, El Caballete, and others overflowing with corpses.

The liberal government did not assume, of course, divine justice as the cause of the epidemic and made all efforts to combat it. The city authorities took extreme measures, such as the prohibition of fruit, vegetables, and even chiles rellenos.

The scenes were repeated day after day; fumigation, vinegar and chloride irrigations, patches stuck to the body, pumpkins with vinegar, solitary pots of rice, and bleedings were a daily occurrence, along with candles in front of images of the saints.

Faith was the population's greatest palliative care, and the salvation of a sick person nourished hopes for the capital's people, who followed the dietary recommendations, remedies, and hygiene measures taken by the sick to avoid the grave. No treatment was completely effective, however, and people had to wait for the epidemic to run its course and disappear. Unfortunately, a cure would only be discovered in the last quarter of the nineteenth century.

Semana Santa

Year after year, for a good part of the nineteenth century, La Semana Santa (Holy Week) disrupted everyday life. Mexico City rose majestic and solemn during this important time. For four days people went from the joy of Maundy Thursday (the institution of the Eucharist) to the sadness of Good Friday (the crucifixion and death of Christ), to the liberating feeling of Holy Saturday, with the burning of Judas. Everything concluded in the infinite joy of Easter Sunday.

An ecclesiastical provision, endorsed by civil authorities, determined for years that from 10 a.m. on Holy Thursday until 10 a.m. on Holy Saturday, the only carriage that could run through the city was the one leading to the "Divinísimo." The sepulchral silence, in accordance with the approaching mourning, overtook ever-faithful Mexico City.

With the streets closed, citizens enjoyed the city's beauty and took advantage of the obligatory stroll from one church to another. In those hot days, there was no shortage of traditional flavored water. Year after year stalls set up in the most crowded places offered a few minutes of refreshment to passersby.

Holy Week also gave free rein to vanity. At the end of the 1830s, the Marchioness Calderón de la Barca wrote: "Maundy Thursday is a day in which Mexico takes on a more than picturesque gaiety. Only satin and velvet are worn on this day, and pearls and diamonds are thrown into the street."

Fireworks could be heard from the early hours of Holy Saturday announcing the burning of Judas that took place on Calle Tacuba. According to Artemio de Valle Arizpe, the Judas tradition had its origins in colonial times:

> The inquisition brought out grotesque figures made of cardboard and armed with reeds or cloth representing inmates who had died, and burned them in effigy. . . . Children playing did similar things; they undertook pretend acts of faith with dolls that they took to a bonfire supposedly for heretics. Since the Inquisition, the figures traditionally portrayed Judas Iscariot, with whom they wanted to personify the Jews, opponents of the Catholic religion. They found this entertaining, and the rag dolls began to be sold in the Merchants' Gate, with ugly faces, beards, horns, and long, bull-like tails. In the same way the traitorous apostle hung himself, the ugly dolls were hanged, and instead of being thrown into a bonfire, as the children did, they stuffed them with fireworks so they would burn, in a simulation of the imagined punishment for the nefarious betrayal by bearded Judas.

143

Mexico City ended Easter between solemnity and celebration but unwaveringly maintained its majesty and the seriousness of the religious act. At dusk on Easter Sunday, after listening to mass and strolling through the popular festivities, people retired to their homes to enjoy a cup of chocolate and share their Holy Week experiences.

In towns near the city, holy days were lived in a more intense way. In San Ángel, Coyoacán, and Iztapalapa, the Passion of Christ was represented with all the frenzy that flourished among the people who wished to play a role in the historical religious drama. They dressed up in roles that best suited them and hoped for an opportunity to accompany Jesus in his terrible fate. Through the streets of Coyoacán and Tacubaya walked Jews, Pharisees, centurions, virgins, apostles, Judas, Pontius Pilate, and Christs who, for an instant, turned the Mexican towns into the Jerusalem of the Christian era's first years.

The large amounts of pulque that flowed in those days unleashed bitterness and quarrels among many villagers. The scene of Christ's apprehension, far from evoking the suffering in the garden of Gethsemane, became a pitched battle where the apostles and other supporters of Jesus fought with Judas and his followers. Although at times the apostles' victory was clear, the result was still the apprehension of Christ, but not without some heavy casualties among his enemies.

Jesus did not fare any better; except for the nails, he suffered almost as much as the true Christ. "It will be a miracle if he survives this day's labors," the astonished Marchioness Calderón de la Barca wrote, after witnessing that the person chosen to revive Christ literally went through "[the labors] of Cain." He certainly suffered horrors, but in the end, like Jesus, he defeated death and rose from the dead amid the crowd's jubilation.

Far from any devotion, the city's inhabitants found in the town of Tlalpan a place to have fun and sin as God intended. On holy days, San Agustín de las Cuevas, as Tlalpan was also known, became Mexico's Las Vegas. It was the only place where gambling and partying were allowed.

There was no reprieve, not even a minute to rest; everything was a huge party from Maundy Thursday to Easter Sunday. Even the humble people contributed to a kitty and sent a representative to Tlalpan in hopes that they would win big playing cards or betting on cockfights. Around 1839 the Marchioness Calderón de la Barca wrote:

> San Agustín de las Cuevas, upon hearing your name, how many hearts beat with emotion! What hands mechanically search empty pockets? How many visions of ounces of gold, gone forever, do not pass before the anguished eyes? How do you hear again the muffled crowing of wounded roosters? What strumming of guitars and the sound of trumpets are heard again!

Life goes on

In the middle of the nineteenth century, daily life in Mexico City was confined to the current historic center. To learn about political life, it was possible to acquire such publications as the *Nineteenth Century*, the *Universal*, the *Order*, and the *Monitor*. Social issues, culture, and good manners appeared in weeklies like *Family Museum*, the *Illustration*, and *Women's Weekly*.

At the beginning of the 1850s, Lake Texcoco still showed its legendary beauty. Several steamship companies provided a service to navigate the great mirror of water that reflected the volcanoes, Popocatépetl and Iztaccíhuatl.

People who wished to take the stagecoach to Tlalpan had to board it on San Agustín Street; if the trip was to San Ángel and Coyoacán, "it leaves daily from the café on the Street of the Ladies and returns the same day: the price of a round-trip seat, one peso." The bus to Chapultepec and Tacubaya left from Callejón de Dolores.

For those who did not like to leave the city, it was common to walk down Calle San Francisco, enjoy the Alameda, or stroll along Paseo de Alameda, Paseo de Bucareli, or Paseo de las Cadenas next to the cathedral. The most popular theaters were the Principal and the National, located on Vergara (today Allende and 5 de Mayo), where opera companies from Europe performed. There were two bullrings, and it was possible to attend the circus erected on Bucareli.

High society met in fashionable cafés such as El Progreso, La Bella Unión, Gran Sociedad, or El Bazar, all located on streets near the College of San Ildefonso. People of limited means could save a few royals and go to the inn at 18 Tlapaleros (today Avenida 16 de Septiembre), better known as the Moor of Venice.

During those years, events attracted citizens' attention, including establishment of the first telegraph line from the capital to the Port of Veracruz, construction of the Mexico–Veracruz railway, and transfer of the famous equestrian statue of Carlos IV (El Caballito) from the University of Mexico courtyard, an operation that took more than a week. At the behest of Don Mariano Arista, president of the Republic, a third door in the National Palace was opened, named the "Marian door" in his honor. Citizens were also surprised by the first ascents in a balloon from the Alameda.

"Extraordinary correspondence from the English Packet" was Mexico's first telegraph message, sent from the capital to Nopalucan, Puebla.

The great national decade

Toward the middle of the nineteenth century, Brantz Mayer, secretary of the U.S. legation in Mexico, wrote: "When I arrived in Mexico, I was told that if I did not stay here for some time I would probably miss the three great Mexican amusements, namely, a revolution, an earthquake, and a bullfight."

Although the country's capital offered a wide range of amusements, the political situation drove people away from the theater and made it difficult for theatrical, musical, and operatic companies to survive.

With Santa Anna's fall in 1855 and the rise of the liberal generation led by Benito Juárez, the country entered into a definitive war between Liberals and Conservatives lasting ten years, including the fight against the French intervention and Maximilian's empire, known as the Second War of Independence.

At the beginning of the liberal era (1855), the capital had three first-rate theaters—the National, the Principal, and the New Mexico—and several theaters of lesser quality that became meeting places for high society, including the Mexican Pavilion, where different *pastorelas* with suggestive names such as *Eternal*

War on Mortals by the Infernal Furies were shown. The Theater of Progress or New Post, also called the Orient, had been built long before in a cowshed, as had the Clock, located on the street of the same name. There was also the Olympic Circus, where an equestrian troupe directed by José Soledad Aycardo, also known as Don Chole, performed.

During the Great National Decade (1857–67), so called because the Liberals fought against the conservative agenda of French intervention and the Maximilian empire, cultural life had to overcome the chaotic situation, especially in the theater, and survive the call for war. Entrepreneurs' imagination to bring entertainment and make money, however, had no limits.

In February 1858 the Great Aerial Theater, a recreation center, opened in the Jupiter Tonante temple, where bad companies appeared with low-cost tickets so ordinary people could attend; an exhibition of balloons and other events were also announced for the distraction of the public.

Mexico City was not a war zone, except when the Liberal troops, under the command of Gen. José Santos Degollado, attempted to lay siege to it in April 1859; they were defeated at Tacubaya. The capital was completely calm, trying to maintain a sense of normalcy.

Due to low incomes and poor ticket sales, the Italian opera company formed by Adelaida Cortesi proposed an event she called a "grand concert," *Promenade à la Parisienne*, which premiered on November 1, 1858, and was announced as follows:

> The show will last from 6 p.m. to midnight: the theater will be arranged as a magnificent hall with double illumination and in such a way that the audience can enjoy the entertainment in comfort. All the artists of the company, the choirs, the orchestra, and the bands hired for the show will take part in the concert. And the portico will be transformed into a beautiful garden.

It was a kind of massive nonstop concert that turned out to be quite a novelty and was repeated days later.

Ducks to water

In the 1860s Don Sebastián Pane introduced traditional wells into Mexico in order to construct public baths in the capital. His entrepreneurial vision, however, went even further: he had the agency to build a swimming pool so residents could escape the high temperatures of spring and summer.

On Sunday, March 13, 1864, two months before Maximilian and Carlota's arrival, the press announced the sensational show being prepared at the Pane pool, which included a water jousting act on boats, a floating table on which a sailor would carve a turkey, a Newfoundland dog that would wrestle with a Mexican dog in the water, trapeze acts, a swimming bed and a floating bottle for those who were thirsty, and hunting a pig in the water by grabbing it by the tail.

The Pane pool was equipped with various objects for swimmers' pleasure—rings, trapezes, and diving boards. There was no shortage of exhibitions by characters such as Colorado, who dove for several minutes without taking a breath, causing the public to fear for his life, and Charrondo, who ate fruit and candy from the bottom of the pool.

The Pane pool was located in what is now the Juárez neighborhood, on Calle Atenas between Versalles and Abraham González Streets.

155

Blushing

After the empire's fall and the Republic's triumph in 1867, the event that most attracted attention in Mexico City was the arrival of the cancan.

Gaztambide's company premiered *The Gods from Olympus* in Mexico on June 22, 1869, and there was an arrangement of *Orpheus in the Underworld* by Jacques Offenbach. "That was the victorious entry of the cancan in Mexico," wrote Enrique de Olavarría y Ferrari. The audience at the first show was astounded. No one in the country had ever seen such a spectacle, and soon the news of what this dance was all about spread like wildfire.

The show provoked mixed feelings and sparked great controversy. Morality and decency did not take long to appear. For many critics, it was vulgar entertainment that brought out people's most primitive instincts, being performed in all kinds of theaters, from the National to the *jacalones* (huts) and improvised tents in public places. The most modest venues, such as the Hidalgo, announced functions where their enthusiastic dancers would perform cancan numbers "remarkable in cheek and dishonesty."

The cancan was by no means a spur-of-the-moment occurrence nor a smoke screen to distract people in times of crisis. It was a sign of changing times, of the modernity of the nineteenth century's last years, of the Belle Époque that flourished in Paris. Yet critics announced the apocalypse: "The dramatic art is in eclipse, in the face of the corrupting spectacle of the zarzuela and the cancan," journalist Ignacio Manuel Altamirano wrote.

The editorials in the press did not leave a puppet with a head; the cancan was a dance with "an exhibition of more or less false calves, unrestrained leaps, lewd and provocative contortions" that fueled lust. The cancan could "make a marble statue blush."

It took French companies a year to succeed in Mexico, and in 1870 every would-be theater manager would have cancan performed at his venue. "It has spread with the speed of cholera," wrote the critic Luis G. Ortiz in 1870. People whistled and sang it, and any criticism was frowned upon by the public. He continued:

> With stupid impudence, they talk about the unbridled cancan circus. At the National or the Principal, the seats that are sold out when it is known that the dancers are going to be sublime with shamelessness and delirium, that their skirts will go up to their necks, and that their partners will reveal in their contortions all the mysteries of incontinence. It is truly strange that people who dance the jarabe have become so passionate about the cancan of whores and unfortunate gypsies.

In addition to the cancan, entrepreneurs did everything possible to bring audiences to the theaters. In 1870 the director of the National Theater found it easy to raise money by hanging sausages, hams, cheeses, and tins of sardines on the trees of a set of the city of Jauja, in the play *The Devil's Auction*. At the end of the play, the food was raffled among the audience, which Altamirano severely criticized:

> Could you have ever imagined a bacon-shop scene at the National Theater? Well, you're seeing it now. It seems that this afternoon they are going to raffle pound cakes at the theater in which Sontag and Salvi, Marini and Peralta have sung.... And yet, the public attends in droves; there is no doubt that the tastes of the Mexican public are becoming more refined every day.

Society sought entertainment, not refinement, and just as the National and the Principal hosted the French companies, other entrepreneurs decided Mexican dancers could also do the cancan. The *jacalón* known as El Olimpo, located in the Alameda, was not far behind; its billboard included cancans and zarzuelas.

> "Here the cancan reaches the unbelievable," noted a February 1875 article. "The shouting and the obscenities reach unprecedented levels; night after night the public and the actors make colossal zambras [flamenco dances], and that, more than theater, is an onstage orgy of wax Venuses from Campeche and brown paper Apollos and Jupiters."

By the end of the 1870s, the cancan could claim victory. It had defeated good conscience.

Modern times

The winds of modernization began to blow strongly over Mexico in 1876, when Porfirio Díaz became president of the Republic for the first time. For the people, accustomed to the ups and downs of politics and war, the new government was just one more. No one could have foreseen the great transformation the country would undergo: order, peace, and progress—Don Porfirio's patriotic obsession—would determine the nation's destiny for the next thirty-five years.

Under Porfirio Díaz, the Republic's capital transformed like never before. A francophilia in architecture, fashion, and lifestyle took hold of noble and loyal Mexico City and the rest of the country. Major public works were completed, and others were started. Don Porfirio succeeded in maintaining political order, and material progress knocked on Mexico's doors.

The capital saw unprecedented economic growth. Foreign investment began to arrive in Mexico; mining was reactivated, factory smoke replaced the smoke from cannons, and oil production became the industrial activity of the new century; banks opened their doors in different parts of the country, and department stores such as the Port of Liverpool, the Palacio de Hierro (iron palace), and the Port of Veracruz multiplied.

The Port of Veracruz was located at the corner of Monterilla and Capuchinas, today 5 de Febrero and Venustiano Carranza.

The cities began to show a different side—that of electric lights and asphalted streets; of the telegraph, efficient mail, and the telephone; of carriages that gave way to the first automobiles in 1896.

At the end of the nineteenth century, Don Porfirio put the novel electric tramway into service, which gradually replaced mule-drawn streetcars. In 1900 he initiated a drainage works project in the Valley of Mexico and construction of the Federal District Penitentiary, known as Lecumberri. Two years later

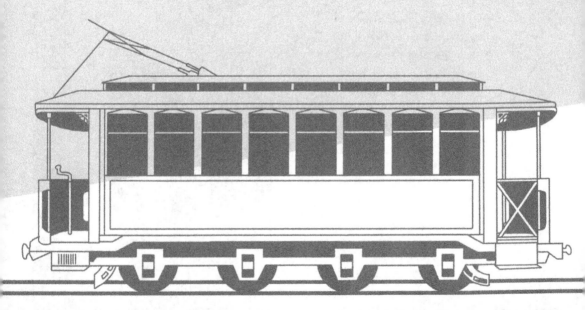

he laid the first stone of the Independence Monument, which would be crowned with a winged victory. Also in 1902, the Mexican Gas and Electric Light Company promoted the city's beautification by introducing underground wiring to replace the unsightly outside poles and wires. Between 1905 and 1910 other projects were started, including the Lagunilla Market, a slaughterhouse, the General Hospital, the Hospice of the Poor, La Castañeda asylum, the Palace of Communications, and the Post Office Building.

La Castañeda asylum was founded on land that was once a pulque plantation in the town of Mixcoac.

There was no doubt that in their leisure time, people indulged with a true festive spirit in the amusements and entertainment options the city offered in the last quarter of the nineteenth century and the first decade of the twentieth. These distractions ranged from outings to and from the capital to an endless number of novel shows in different venues.

The attendance of different social classes at the theater, opera, puppet shows, circus, bullfighting, and cockfighting—already part of a long tradition dating back to the viceregal era—continued during independent Mexico, but with the idea of "modernity" that burst into Mexico at the end of the nineteenth century. It was a modernity that brought electricity, the telephone, the automobile, the cinematograph, and the phonograph, all reflected in the shows.

Past and future merged in the present. People could go to the traditional theater or be amazed by the first cinematograph. They could attend cockfights and then enjoy one of the kites set up in the Alameda, gather to admire a ventriloquist, or marvel at the first public demonstrations of the phonograph.

Public spaces

Before the end of the nineteenth century, Mexico City had about 450,000 inhabitants. People of high society spent the summer in country houses they had built in Tacubaya, Mixcoac, San Ángel, Coyoacán, and Tlalpan; the middle class and those with limited resources took day trips to these towns on weekends.

One of Mexico City's most popular outings was a visit to the Zócalo. Since the beginning of his administration, Porfirio Díaz's government had offered concerts there on Mondays, Wednesdays, Fridays, and Sundays. Public spaces became popular, and as the gaps in social class increased during the regime, high society stopped attending the Plaza Mayor to listen to music, "for fear of rubbing shoulders with the prostitutes," as González Navarro pointed out.

Until Don Porfirio came to power, the Alameda Central was an exclusive promenade for the most select of Mexican society; even admission was charged. In 1881 city authorities built a rotunda illuminated by electric lights and with seating for up to three thousand, in which concerts were held on Sundays. This led to the Alameda becoming a typical venue for the middle class and the busiest during the entire administration.

During Díaz's second presidential term (1884–88), it was ordered that the Moorish Pavilion, built for the Universal Exhibition of 1884, be placed in the Alameda, where the Juárez

Chamber stands today. It soon became a center of attraction for children because of the dances performed there.

The Alameda was a place for music and entertainment. Thousands walked the centuries-old grove on Saturdays and Sundays to listen to *sones*, polkas, waltzes, and military marches. Classical music also had its place, and toward the end of the nineteenth century orchestras performed Franz von Suppé's *Fatinitza March*, Rossini's *Barber of Seville* overture, Tomás León's polka-mazurka *Catalina*, Donizetti's *Maria di Rohan*, and national pieces such as the Lindas Mexicanas march, the Alejandra waltz, Abundio Martínez's paso doble *Hidalguense*, and Juventino Rosas's famous *Sobre las olas*.

Vendors of toys, ice cream, soft drinks, and candy shared the space with cedars, bluebells, chrysanthemums, lilies, dahlias, roses, geraniums, daisies, petunias, and laurels from India, all in an immaculate environment thanks to the Guardians Corps of the Commission of Walks, who swept and watered the place ten times a day.

The Alameda had a skating rink, in operation since 1895, with different times for women and for men. Ladies could skate, in dresses, from Tuesday to Friday until 1 p.m. The men's shift began at 4 p.m. and lasted until late at night.

The euphoria for riding bicycles was unleashed in 1892, and by 1896 there were eight hundred bicycles in the capital. Women also enjoyed cycling, although at first it was frowned upon as a "tomboyish" activity not in keeping with decency and good feminine mores.

The most famous circus at the end of the nineteenth century was the Orrin, which some said was not a business but a public institution, a custom as deeply rooted as Easter and the Posadas, a simulation of Mary and Joseph asking for a room at the inn. It is the core of the Mexican people's joyful tradition in which performers such as the clown Ricardo Bell became famous.

The theater was also transformed. The revue theater, with Mexican characters like the gendarme, the worker, the bald man, and the drunk, began in 1904 with the successful *Chin-Chun-Chan*'s premier at the Teatro Principal. It ran uninterrupted from 1904 to 1942, reaching ten thousand performances throughout the country and becoming the country's most popular music comedy.

The cinematograph's arrival in Mexico in 1896 was undoubtedly the great novelty of the time. On August 6, 1896, Don Porfirio and his family enjoyed the first screening at a private performance at the Chapultepec Castle. One of the first films shown in Mexico featured Díaz himself. A successful public function for the press was subsequently held on the Plateros drugstore's upper floors.

Paseo de la Reforma

In addition to the Zócalo and the Alameda, people strolled along San Francisco and Plateros (today
Avenida Madero) and the Plaza de Santo Domingo.
Other public spaces were the gardens of San Francisco, Paseo de Bucareli, the Tivolis of San Cosme, the
Tivolis of Eliseo, the Petit Versailles, and the Chateau
des Fleurs, among others. Perhaps the busiest of all
was Paseo de la Reforma.

Conceived as a twelve-kilometer-long boulevard
linking Chapultepec and Paseo de Bucareli, it had
been laid out during Maximilian's empire under the
name Paseo del Emperador. With the Republic's triumph, the avenue acquired its definitive name, Paseo
de la Reforma.

Development of the paseo was dizzying. Between
1872 and 1902 it transformed along with the city's
urban landscape. The government began its expansion by adding sidewalks with benches and planting
different tree species. In 1877 the Christopher Colum-
bus Monument was inaugurated on the second roundabout, followed ten years later by the Cuauhtémoc
Monument. That same year a bullring was built at the
paseo's entrance, but it was unsuccessful and was demolished soon after.

From the 1880s on, development of adjacent colonies like Cuauhtémoc and Juárez, which became two of the most important of the Porfiriature, began. At the decade's end, in 1889, the famous Café Colón opened its doors, becoming a meeting place for the high Porfirian society.

The paseo's beautification was complemented by a series of statues placed along the avenue, which remain today, and in 1891, as if guarding the entrance, two monumental sculptures were installed, evoking the pre-Hispanic past and becoming known as Indios Verdes. They were rejected by the public and removed shortly after. In 1902 the Independence Monument's first stone was laid.

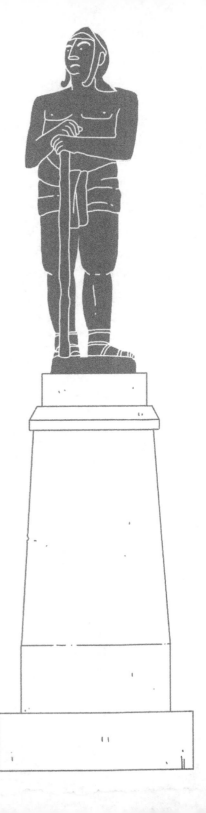

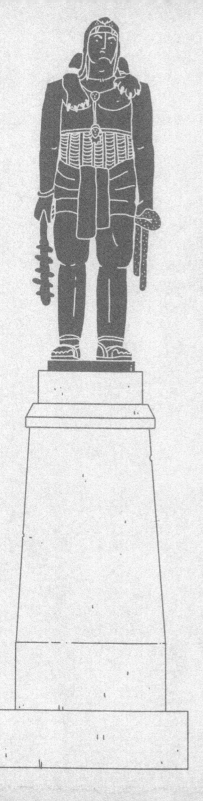

In just a few years, the paseo became a place where society gathered to admire the parades of allegorical floats in different festivities throughout the year and participate in the flower fights, when people threw flowers at each other, either as a symbol of friendship or to make clear some boy's interest in a young girl; to go horseback riding; or to applaud the bicycle and automobile races. Cafés like Colón were favored by a large clientele who liked to walk the sidewalks or take carriages or trams to Chapultepec forest, which also regained its former splendor once Porfirio Díaz established his summer residence in the Chapultepec Castle.

The Porfiriate's air of modernity displaced several pastimes that had long been accepted and enjoyed by the capital's society. The main one was the capital's carnival, which was consigned to history, though it resurfaced with new vigor in different states of the Republic.

If the festivities that announced the arrival of Lent since the viceregal period were cause for celebration, jubilation, and more than a few excesses, from 1878 on they became infrequent, disappearing completely in Mexico City by the beginning of the twentieth century.

Parades, popular dances, and masquerades gave way to typical customs from France like the flower fights in Paseo de la Reforma and surrounding towns such as Mixcoac and San Ángel. People stopped attending the dances, which, under the pretext of the carnival, were organized in theaters such as the National, the Arbeu, and the Principal.

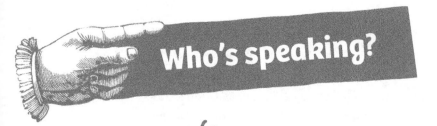

Who's speaking?

¡RING, RING!

Established at 6 Santa Isabel, now Bellas Artes, in 1891 the Mexican Telephone Company had more than a thousand subscribers who enjoyed the telephone's benefits. Years earlier, on March 15, 1878, Tlalpan had become the first town in the Republic to receive a telephone call from Mexico City.

Thirteen years later the Mexican Telephone Company published its first subscriber list, announcing that "the price for every new line will be six pesos and twenty-five cents per month for lines of a kilometer or less. An additional ten pesos will be charged for installation costs."

Subscribers had the right to "speak with each other whenever they want and with the utmost secrecy. When you tell the Central Office who you want to speak to, say with which number and not with which name." The phone book and subscriber list were only twenty-one pages long and listed all users, regardless of their social status.

President Díaz could be called at number 64. The future minister of finance, José Limantour, had number 62. The Romero Rubio family, Porfirio's in-laws, could be called at 127, the number of their home on Calle San Andrés, or at their mansion in the neighboring town of Tacubaya by dialing 1005. Department stores such as the Port of Liverpool and the Port of Veracruz had similar numbers—643 and 634, respectively—which sometimes caused confusion.

As a "very important" warning, J. E. Torbet, general manager of the Mexican Telephone Company, stated: "The company requests that when two subscribers have concluded their call, each ring his bell so that the two plates may fall at the Central Office as a sign that they have finished. In this way, they are in a position to speak with the other person, and for the other person to speak to them."

Everything was listed in the 1891 phone book: hotels, shops, restaurants, oil companies, factories, railway lines, government departments, public officials, individuals, and at number 1, the only permanently profitable business—Eusebio Gayoso's Funeral Parlor.

The Twentieth Century

Centennial celebrations

In September 1910 Mexico City was dressed in lights. The nation was commemorating the first centennial of its independence, and the Porfirian regime wanted to show the world the progress and growth the Republic had achieved under its government.

The city maintained its customary calm. However, groups of Maderistas protested the imprisonment of Francisco I. Madero, which had occurred the previous June, on the eve of election day, and Porfirio Díaz's triumph in the elections.

As usual, the daily events in the capital unfolded in its historic center. Some businesses stood out from others, and newspapers such as *El Imparcial, El Diario del Hogar,* and *México Nuevo,* among others, filled their pages with advertisements.

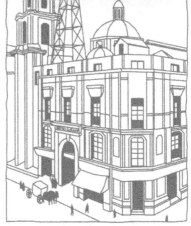

For home decoration, people could go to El Universo, "the great furniture store of Juan Fernandez." To buy the latest fashionable footwear, a visit to the Elephant shoe shop was a must, and smokers could do no better than Partagás on Avenida Isabel la Católica. Music lovers could get sheet music, instruments, and the new double-sided records at Wagner and Levieu on Calle San Francisco.

Several hotels advertised all the comforts—telephones, electric lighting, and private bathrooms—like the Hotel Colón on Avenida Isabel la Católica; the Grand Hotel and Restaurant Barcelona on Avenida 16 de Septiembre; the well-known Hotel Gillow on Isabel la Católica, between Plateros and 5 de Mayo; and the Grand Hotel on Ortega.

Restaurants such as the Gambrinus, La Ópera, and Colón, as well as El Globo candy store, opened their doors to journalists, politicians, people from the theater, and the general public.

In the center, shoppers could find costume jewelry stores, all kinds of leather and furs, bookstores, candy stores, banks, and even funeral parlors offering "fine and ordinary" coffins. Advertisements in the printed press were particularly curious:

> Do you want to be happy and not live with sadness, misery, tormenting worries, without love, without joy, without happiness? Ask today for the means to achieve success in life and get what you want; you can have fortune, health, and luck with my free book titled *Wonderful Secrets*.

From September 1 to October 6, 1910, the city was transformed into a great stage. There were countless events for every social class: openings, fairs, literary and musical evenings, concerts, theater, opera, banquets, tributes, unveilings, dances, processions, and parades filled the Mexican people's leisure hours. The apotheosis was the dedication of the Independence Column, on the morning of September 16, on Paseo de la Reforma.

The revolution

Almost two months after the centennial celebrations' end, on November 20, 1910, the Maderista revolution broke out in the north. The Porfirian government mobilized troops to quell the growing social unrest that threatened the country's stability, but the early stages of the revolution did not alter daily life in Mexico City.

On May 10, 1911, Juárez fell to the revolutionaries, and its immediate consequence was Porfirio Díaz's downfall. On May 25, 1911, after thirty-one years in power, Don Porfirio tendered his resignation to Congress, which was opening its new building at the intersection of Allende and Donceles.

Paradoxically, the Porfiriate's last act took place in the new Chamber of Deputies, on what had been the site of the Iturbide Theater until 1872, when it was handed over to legislators after a fire in the enclosure of the National Palace.

For locals and strangers alike, the strong earthquake that shook Mexico City hours before Madero's entrance into the capital was a harbinger of change. With enormous precision, history showed that such a momentous arrival was only a prelude to great changes: in 1821, with Iturbide, Mexico had begun its independent life; in 1848, after the American occupation, when the city again became the Republic's capital, Mexico sought to redefine its course without half its territory; in 1867 Juárez tenaciously embodied the Republic until the triumph over Maximilian's empire; and, more recently, Díaz had announced the era of peace, order, and progress in 1876. All had found their power and fate in Mexico City.

Madero would not be the exception. On June 7, 1911, the old City of Palaces witnessed a victorious parade. The day marked the end of the nineteenth century for Mexico and its slow march toward the twentieth. Chroniclers, writers, and journalists reported on the massive spontaneous reception the capital's more than one hundred thousand inhabitants gave Madero.

But the honeymoon lasted barely fifteen months. After Madero's inauguration as president, the old political class and military regime conspired to overthrow him, and in the early hours of February 9, 1913, Generals Bernardo Reyes and Félix Díaz were released from prison and took command of a large army. At the same time, the Tlalpan Military Academy and another armed group in Tacubaya marched toward the city center.

The coup's leaders believed they had unobstructed entry into the National Palace, but they were repelled by government forces. General Reyes was left lying in the Plaza Mayor along with dozens of corpses, passed by curious onlookers on their way to the cathedral for the first Sunday mass. The rest of the rebels retreated and made a stronghold in the well-known Citadel building, an arms depot.

Thus began the so-called Tragic Decade, because for ten days—from February 9 to February 18, 1913—the city center and the Juárez and Cuauhtémoc neighborhoods were the scene of terrible fighting between proponents of the coup and forces loyal to Madero. At no other time in its history has Mexico City suffered such destruction from an armed confrontation.

The fighting ended with Madero's and José María Pino Suárez's arrest on February 18 and their assassination on February 22, which took place behind the Lecumberri Penitentiary, opened in 1900. Victoriano Huerta took power on February 19, and a month later the constitutionalist revolution broke out; its leaders would make the capital pay for the insult of supporting the coup against Madero.

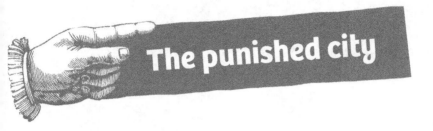

The punished city

The men of the north, the constitutionalists, were clamoring for revenge, first against Huerta for the usurpation and assassination of Madero, and then against Mexico City, because its inhabitants had been accomplices of the coup d'état by allowing the outrage and standing idly by to see Madero fall. But they also claimed a centuries-old affront: northerners had long suffered from centralization, decades when the capital was left with most of the resources and had been the least affected in times of war.

> The whole country is in tatters, and its poor inhabitants have suffered unspeakably with the revolt. Only Mexico City has lost nothing, and yet it is always the cradle of coups and revolutions. It is only fair that this time she should pay for her failings, and we will punish her harshly, just as we will punish all those who helped Huerta.
> — Venustiano Carranza

190

Álvaro Obregón first arrived in Mexico City in the middle of August 1914 after Huerta's resignation a month before. On August 20 Venustiano Carranza paraded victoriously through the capital's streets. Then the revenge began. The mansions of the old Porfirio supporters were confiscated and occupied by Carranza's generals; the mansions of Braniff, Casasús, Nacho de la Torre, and Porfirio Díaz Jr., among many others, were converted into barracks and brothels. The generals drained the wine cellars, destroyed the libraries, and allowed looting by the troops.

The occupation by Carranza's men lasted until the end of November, and for months the city's inhabitants lived in fear.

Villistas and Zapatistas

As is well known, after Huerta's resignation the country did not find peace; it entered a new period of violence. The revolutionaries divided and faced each other in a struggle for power. On one side were Carranza and Obregón; on the other, Villa and Zapata. At the end of 1914, Carranza and his men left the capital and the Villistas and Zapatistas advanced. The city's inhabitants were terrified. If things had gone badly with the constitutionalists, what could they expect from the Villistas and Zapatistas, let alone from their leaders? Villa had a reputation as an assassin, and Zapata was known by the capital's press as the "Attila of the South."

Paradoxically, the Zapatista occupation was orderly. Most of the peasants had never been to a city like the capital, and they toured it with caution and even fear; they were impressed and uncomfortable.

> Not knowing what role they should play, they did not plunder or pillage, but, like lost children, they wandered the streets, knocking on doors and asking for food.
>
> — John Womack

On December 6, 1914, Villa and Zapata made their triumphant entry into the city. About fifty thousand men gathered in Chapultepec, and at 11 a.m. they began to advance along Reforma Avenue. The parade concluded in the Plaza Mayor, where both leaders and their main generals were received at the National Palace by President Eulalio Gutiérrez. There Pancho Villa took a photo that went down in history: he sat in the presidential chair, smiling, accompanied by Zapata, who wasn't.

Villa's presence in Mexico City had its anecdotal moments. He wept bitterly in front of Madero's tomb in the French Pantheon of La Piedad. His affection and admiration for Don Panchito had been sincere, and he renamed the street to pay homage to his hero. Moreover, he swore that he would kill whoever dared to change it again.

For several weeks the capital lived in uncertainty and anxiety. Those difficult months in the capital were the only ones in which society paid for its indifference and lack of commitment.

Villa's permanence in the capital brought discredit and scandal. His officers showed up at the busiest restaurants and drank, ate, and signed vouchers instead of paying. What we saved in a month, Villa and his people spent in one night of orgies.

— José Vasconcelos

Mexico City finally suffered the ravages of the revolution. Many businesses closed, and there was an economic crisis, food shortages, and executions among the revolutionaries. Entertainment also suffered, and most of the theaters, marquees, and squares canceled their performances.

The only artist who faced up to the military occupation in the capital was María Conesa, who at the end of December 1914 returned to the stage after a two-year retirement to appear in a long run at the Teatro Colón. So famous were her performances that the revolutionaries said they had two obligations upon arriving in the city: "to visit the Virgin of Guadalupe at La Villa and María at the Colón."

Peace once more

The country entered a period of relative peace from 1917 to 1920. The revolution's most violent phase had concluded, and although Francisco Villa ravaged some towns in the north, he no longer represented a real threat to the Carranza government. General Pablo González's campaign against the Zapatistas in the south continued and would culminate with Zapata's assassination in 1919.

The capital returned to normal, and for a few months in 1919 the bullrings opened for events that had nothing to do with bullfighting. In February, ballerina Anna Pavlova, with a company of fifty dancers from the Imperial Russian Ballet, made her Mexican debut at the Toreo de la Condesa.

On September 29 the recently opened Teatro Esperanza Iris—today Teatro de

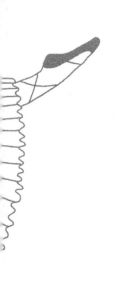

la Ciudad—received a world-renowned figure who caused a furor among the capital's society. That night Enrico Caruso made his Mexican debut in Donizetti's *Elixir of Love*. His success was so great that he extended his performances until the end of October 1919.

The theater wasn't large enough for the public who wanted to hear him, so they set up in the Plaza El Toreo. Caruso and his company performed Bizet's *Carmen* for twenty thousand spectators in the first days of October, in the middle of a torrential downpour. Despite the rain, not a soul moved from the arena. Caruso won the hearts of the people, who crowded into the venues where he performed for more than a month.

> I can declare that I was happy in Mexico, as a man and as a traveler. The weather was delightful; and outside of Italy I have never seen a sky as beautiful and clear as the one of Mexico City. I am told that people who don't have good lungs suffer from the rarified atmosphere here. I had nothing to fear in this regard, and although it seems pointless to mention, I must say that Caruso has good lungs.
>
> — Enrico Caruso

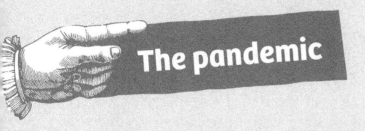

The pandemic

In the last quarter of 1918, the terrible Spanish flu pandemic reached Mexico. The disease entered the northeastern part of the Republic in the first days of October and claimed its first victims in Nuevo Laredo, Tamaulipas, followed by Juárez, Chihuahua, Torreón, and Saltillo in Coahuila.

The first cases in the capital were detected on the outskirts of Villa de Guadalupe. Infection increased rapidly, and by the end of the month the disease had spread throughout the city. The department of health took drastic measures. Trains to infected areas were suspended; cinemas, theaters, clubs, bars, churches, and other places where people gathered were closed to avoid further spread. Even the Basilica of Guadalupe was closed on October 17.

There was no general lockdown; in the city, the government tried to isolate the sick, forbade the sale of street food and kissing, and threatened to fine sick people who left their homes. The use of cotton masks was recommended, and people were ordered not to shake hands. In some cities a curfew was decreed from 11 p.m. to 4 a.m., during which time street sweepers disinfected the streets. Rooms, beds, and everywhere an influenza victim had lived were fumigated.

By October 20, the newspapers announced that in Juárez and other towns, the authorities were unable to bury the corpses. It was the same in the capital. Even though funeral services were banned, people watched over their deceased in the streets, waiting for a vehicle to pass to collect the bodies. Coffins piled up daily in the center.

Infection began to decrease in the first half of December. In two and a half months, the city's death toll had reached twelve thousand. The influenza pandemic caused nearly half a million deaths nationwide.

The Roaring Twenties

The second decade of the twentieth century was one of the most violent; war, famine, and disease claimed a million Mexicans. By 1910 the face of Mexico had been transformed. In the census of 1921, Mexicans numbered just over 14 million while the capital's population increased. If in 1910 it had 720,000 inhabitants, toward 1921 it had reached 900,000, of which 615,000 were located in Mexico City and the rest in Azcapotzalco, Coyoacán, San Ángel, Tlalpan, and other municipalities.

Two large, unfinished structures towered above the rest of the city's buildings as a vestige of the times of Porfirio Díaz: the new National Theater, now the Bellas Artes, awaited government approval to continue construction; and the Monument to the Revolution, an abandoned metal structure of what was never to become the great legislative palace.

Electric trams, passenger buses, and automobiles had almost entirely replaced horse-drawn carriages, which were prohibited from using the asphalt streets beginning in 1927. Even the stables of the National Palace were transformed into garages for official cars. In 1921 the *Excelsior* newspaper reported that 16,127 cars, 2,555 trucks, and 429 motorcycles were circulating in the city.

Women's fashion changed radically from the last years of the Porfiriate. The corset disappeared, and the new straight

and loose dresses made women's curves disappear. Dress lengths reached a little below the knee, showing women's calves, which caused a great scandal. What caused the biggest furor, however, was that women began to wear their hair short. It didn't take long for Catholic groups to protest. A song of the time noted:

No more baldheads
no more presumption
whoever wants to be a flapper
pays a contribution.

Flapper referred to modern women who wore their hair and skirts short. They were jazz fanatics and were independently sexual, and many had political opinions.

In addition to traditional neighborhoods such as Cuauhtémoc and Juárez, new ones began to be added, such as the Lomas de Chapultepec residential project (1923), the neighborhood of Chapultepec (1925), Polanco (1926), Hipódromo Condesa (1926), where horse races were held, and the neighborhoods of Colonia del Valle, Santa María, Guerrero, San Rafael, and Industrial.

Everyday events continued to develop with more impetus in the city center: business and commerce, culture and art, politics, and intellectual life. Daytime and nighttime activities brought life to the downtown streets. People frequented Café Tacuba, La Flor de México, Sanborn's of the Tiles, Selecty, and Café América. Politicians met at El Prendes, on Avenida 16 de Septiembre, a stone's throw away from the National Palace, which was the seat of executive power, and from the Chamber of Deputies in the former Iturbide Theater on Donceles.

Of Dutch origin, Mata Hari was an exotic dancer and spy during World War I. She never set foot in Mexico, but her reputation was well known in these parts.

Nighttime cabaret

In the years of reconstruction, Mexico City suddenly gave way to nightlife. It was no longer just about the theater, cafés, and cinemas. The time had come for dancing and debauchery. Salón México, known as El Marro, opened on April 20, 1921, and was located in the Guerrero neighborhood on the corner of Pensador Mexicano and 2nd of April. It came to be considered the cathedral of *danzón*, and its dances and contests defined an era. Great orchestras appeared there. Such was its fame that it inspired Aaron Copland's symphonic work *El Salón México* and the celebrated 1948 film of the same name, directed by Emilio "El Indio" Fernández.

The Mata Hari dance hall, open from 1917 to 1929, was a cabaret on the second floor of a large house at the corner of Bolívar and Madero, on the same street where the Teatro Principal was located. Night owls, after attending a performance, could continue the party with drinks there. At first only soft drinks were sold, and eventually wine and liquor. Neighbors protested patrons' raucous behavior and finally managed to get the venue closed in 1929.

Steak sandwiches, in giant rolls, with potato, avocado, beans, cream, lettuce, tomato, and lots of salsa, became famous at the Cabaret Conchita, which operated from 1915 to 1930 at 127 República de El Salvador, on the corner of Callejón Parque del Conde. Guests could either enjoy the famous sandwich for twelve cents or dance with the girls for five cents a dance.

In the 1920s a place that even today attracts a large and faithful following established its reputation. Around 1919 the capital's press reported that a group of musicians from Cocula, Jalisco, met in the Pila Seca plaza to sing songs. They used a name that was uncommon at the time—mariachis.

In 1921 the Pila was renamed Garibaldi Plaza to honor Giuseppe Garibaldi, grandson of the Italian hero, who joined the revolution and fought alongside Madero in 1911. Around 1923 the plaza was surrounded by modest shops, a market, pulque bars, neighborhoods, and Tenampa, a cantina owned by Juan Hernández. Its success was instantaneous, and the public found in Garibaldi Plaza entertainment closer to the new Mexicanness favored by the postrevolutionary governments.

Other centenary celebrations

On December 1, 1920, Álvaro Obregón became president. The new government came up with the idea of commemorating the first centenary of independence in 1921 with a series of parties and popular events to give it a different flavor from those organized by Porfirio Díaz's government in 1910.

The celebrations were a joke. Mexico was going through a terrible economic period, public coffers were empty, and the roads had been destroyed after so many years of war. Society was still polarized by Carranza's assassination in 1920, and the United States did not recognize the new administration. No one was able to stop the centennial project, however. September was accompanied by great receptions, banquets, and parties, but with a popular feel.

> The excitement of the festivities intoxicated the city and dazzled the Republic.
>
> — José Vasconcelos

There was opera. A fan and practitioner of bel canto was in charge of the programming—former president Adolfo de la Huerta. There were popular festivals in the Zócalo and Mexican Nights in Chapultepec forest. Children's Week was commemorated September 11–17 with conferences, exhibitions, and children's festivals, and on September 15 more than seventy thousand children from schools in the Republic pledged allegiance to the flag.

For one week, movies and plays were free, and tens of thousands of tickets were sold at low prices so that workers could attend with their families. There were military parades, popular music in the main squares, bullfights, and sports.

The celebrations for the centennial did not have the importance, luxury, and impact of those of 1910. They were days of entertainment for the people and nothing more. A few days later, Congress removed Iturbide's name in gold letters from the chamber's wall of honor.

The events of the Plan of Iguala and the Iturbide proclamation were not commemorated, nor were they commemorated in the years that followed. That centenary was an expensive joke.

— José Vasconcelos

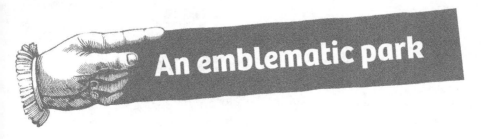

An emblematic park

Revolutionary modernity, driven by the governments of Obregón and Elías Calles in the 1920s, was to be identified with concrete, drainage, electric lighting, and the automobile; with avenues whose median strips would be filled with leafy trees; and with smaller construction sites that would be better utilized.

The middle class claimed its place in history, as the engine of the revolution, and from 1924 on occupied the new and soon to be famous Hippodrome neighborhood, which was built over one of the symbols of Porfirian lavishness and squandering—the Condesa racetrack, owned by the Jockey Club.

The Hippodrome-Condesa neighborhood broke all of the established molds in the city. Architect José Luis Cuevas, who was in charge of the project, designed the neighborhood based on the old racetrack's elliptical shape.

If the Alameda had been the grand promenade of viceregal Mexico and Chapultepec forest had given the Mexico of Don Porfirio the dignity only nature can offer, then revolutionary modernity needed a place for the middle class where everyday life communed with nature, material progress, and the future.

On August 31, 1926, the Federal District Council announced optimistically:

> The large park that [is] being built in the old hippodrome of the Condesa is, surely, one that will be called the first in the capital, since its surface is much larger than that of the Alameda Central and, furthermore, will constitute a true beauty of the metropolis, for its originality and modernism.

The project, dubbed Parque México, was "modern and elegant," according to chroniclers of the late 1920s. Its interior featured art deco elements, the artistic fashion in vogue. Only in the mechanistic and functionalist world of those years was it possible to imagine that a radio clock, placed in a tower in the park, could be a distraction for young and old alike.

> Come. Bring your entire family. Without getting out of your car you will be able to hear perfectly, because our column is powerful enough to be heard 500 meters away.

Art deco could be seen in other parts of the city, including the Ermita in Tacubaya, the building now occupied by the Museum of Popular Art on Calle Revillagigedo, and the Mier y Pesado Institute on Calzada de Guadalupe.

Passersby could spend long hours admiring La Muñeca (the doll), the large art deco fountain depicting a nude woman holding a pitcher in each arm, through which water flowed. The children amused themselves by teasing the guard, then casting their small homemade nets and fishing in the pond.

Worthy of attention is the open-air theater that evokes the open forums of ancient Greece. Its construction coincided with Charles Lindbergh's crossing of the Atlantic in his plane, the *Spirit of Saint Louis*. Dwight Morrow, the American ambassador to Mexico, invited the American pilot to Mexico to demonstrate that relations between the two countries were going well, after tension caused by a thorny oil issue.

Lindbergh left Washington on December 13, 1927, and arrived in Mexico City the next day. The reception was warm, and even the president showed up at the

Balbuena plains to welcome him. The daring pilot received the keys to the city and was declared a guest of honor. To commemorate his visit, the capital's city council, in its January 10, 1928, session, established that "by virtue of the benefits brought to our Republic by the nonstop flight from Washington to Mexico, conducted recently by aforementioned aviator, [it wishes to recognize him by] naming after him the new outdoor theater currently under construction in the Hippodrome-Condesa."

Lindbergh is said to have landed very close to the Parque México, on Avenida Hipódromo (today Avenida Amsterdam), for from the sky he could clearly see the outline of the circuit the Porfirian horses ran around.

To keep Parque México clean, the city council bet on education, good manners, and the civic spirit of the residents and visitors. Signs posted along the paths were real classes in grammar and writing:

THROWING GARBAGE OR FRUIT PEELS SAYS A LOT ABOUT ONE'S SENSE OF CULTURE AND MANNERS.

H AYTO 1927

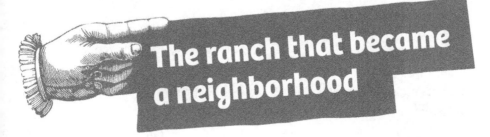

The ranch that became a neighborhood

The Morales Ranch covered a large area of land to the city's west. With the passage of time its lands were demarcated, and in the third decade of the twentieth century it gave rise to one of the capital's most famous neighborhoods—Polanco.

Around 1930, Homero and Horacio Avenues were dirt roads that bordered cornfields, and on Avenida Paredón, now Archimedes, there were only stables. Avenida Julio Verne was the entrance to the Polanco estate on Paseo de la Reforma and Champs-Élysées. Avenida Presidente Masaryk or, as it was known then, Calzada de la Piedra Redonda, was the main road to the ranch. In the original plans this causeway was to be called Avenida Salomon, but Lázaro Cárdenas intervened in 1936 to have it named after the first president and founder of the Republic of Czechoslovakia, thus expressing his support for democracy when fascist totalitarianism ruled in the world.

Polanco emerged as an exclusive residential area; military families arrived because Cárdenas ordered construction of the Official Residence of Los Pinos near the secretary of defense and the military hospital. Later, Jews, Spanish, Germans, Lebanese, and Israelis, who had left the historic center in search of a more exclusive environment, arrived. Wealthy Mexican industrialist families, cattle ranchers, farmers, and miners, especially from the north of the country, also settled there. They transformed Polanco into what it is today.

Champs-Élysées was the course of the river that bounded and irrigated the fields of Morales Ranch. The river crossed the Anzures neighborhood, ended at the Circuito Interior, went down Calzada de la Verónica, and passed the Río Consulado before arriving at Lake Texcoco. The best mansions of the time were erected there, properties reflecting the country's economic boom.

In the same decade, Miguel Alemán Valdés partnered with Gabriel Ramos Millán, Raúl López Sánchez, and Fernando Casas Alemán in the real estate business. They acquired ranchland between the Anzures plains and Rancho de La Hormiga, which became Los Pinos. This is how Polanco Ranch was born and formed the Anzures and Polanco neighborhoods.

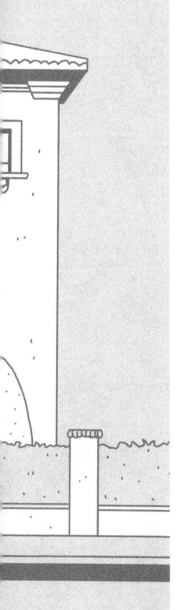

An important innovation in the approach by José de la Lama and Raúl Basurto for the Chapultepec-Polanco estate's layout was to replace the traditional market with a shopping area.

Between 1925 and 1955, the predominant architectural style of Polanco's first houses was Californian, that is, the style of Hollywood mansions. Society turned its attention to the area because it was both fashionable and cheaper to build there than in Las Lomas de Chapultepec, formerly Chapultepec Heights, at that time the city's most exclusive and distant neighborhood.

Infrastructure

From its founding in the sixteenth century to the third decade of the twentieth century, Mexico City retained, to a greater or lesser extent, its natural boundaries. Chapultepec forest toward the west marked the city's end, and between that point and the city center, there were three important neighborhoods: Juárez, Cuauhtémoc, and Guerrero. To the north, past working-class neighborhoods such as Tepito and La Lagunilla, which were part of the center, was Villa de Guadalupe; to the east, San Lázaro and Candelaria de los Patos; and toward the south, Colonia Doctores. Beyond were the towns of Tacubaya, San Ángel, Coyoacán, Tlalpan, and Xochimilco.

Unprecedented urban growth beginning in the 1930s peaked during the presidency of Miguel Alemán (1946–52), who encouraged an urban transformation that had not been seen since the times of Díaz.

Mixcoac, San Ángel, Coyoacán, and Tlalpan were incorporated into Mexico City when the government united the four cardinal points with important avenues that defined the capital's urban layout. The most important of these were the expansion of Paseo de la Reforma, unification of Avenida de los Insurgentes, the Tlalpan causeway, the Miguel Aleman viaduct, the Periférico ring road, and the axis roads.

Reform again

Ever since Maximilian came up with the idea, Paseo de la Emperatriz (today Paseo de la Reforma) was destined to be one of the capital's iconic avenues, in addition to being Mexico's most beautiful avenue, especially its original three kilometers, which extend from Paseo de Bucareli to the entrance of Chapultepec forest, where Estela de Luz—the monument commemorating the bicentennial of independence—goes almost unnoticed in front of the city's two largest skyscrapers, the Torre Mayor and the BBVA building. The capital's history is encapsulated in those three kilometers' development, transformations, and milestones.

The original layout was extended throughout the twentieth century. In the 1920s almost ten kilometers were built to the west for practical reasons: the city needed an expressway that would lead to the Toluca exit, and toward Chapultepec Heights and Polanco, the two new exclusive neighborhoods.

Another extension—a little more than two kilometers—was built in the 1960s, on the opposite side and heading toward the northeast, from the Reforma and Bucareli roundabouts to the Peralvillo roundabout, where the Los Misterios and Guadalupe causeways began. Between 1948 and 1949, Fernando Casas Alemán, regent of the Federal District, authorized an unprecedented remodeling of the traditional promenade, the biggest thus far.

The flying double buttresses that had been installed in the early 1940s, replacing the Berlin-style light fixtures that illuminated the promenade from the beginning of the twentieth century, had divided the avenue's central lanes for decades. The buttresses were removed, and a median strip was built in their place. To maintain the nationalist spirit, why not decorate the median strip with cacti, nopal, and bishop's-weed? Even before the nopal was fully planted, people began calling it Paseo de la Nopalera. At the beginning of the twenty-first century, the median strip was transformed again and generated a similar controversy, due to the structures, called "the dinosaur tail," placed there.

To accommodate the disproportionate increase in automobiles, the wide meridians from El Caballito roundabout to the Cuauhtémoc Monument were reduced to a width of two meters, barely enough space to allow room for vehicles in the side lanes without having to move the statues of heroes of La Reforma, placed there during the Porfiriate.

The quarry benches in this section were relocated to the stretch between the Cuauhtémoc Monument and the Diana the Huntress statue. The monument to the last Mexica emperor was moved to the intersection of Reforma and Insurgentes, where it remained for several decades. The splendor of this old Porfirian roundabout disappeared completely and, although in 2004 the emperor's statue was returned to its original site, not even the memory of this beautiful roundabout remains, only of the trolley car that passes daily in front of the last *tlatoani* (ruler).

Paseo de la Reforma was the scene of many great events in Mexico City, including military parades like the one on the September 16 holiday, cultural parades such as the Day of the Dead, hot air balloons that were inflated beside the Angel of Independence, concerts, bike rides, a Formula 1 car show, zombie walks and other pop culture events, political demonstrations like the student movement of 1968 and the 2006 reform sit-in, protests around public safety in 2004, the protest of Ayotzinapa in 2014, and the LGBTIQ+ movement marches.

The Boy Heroes take Reforma

On September 27, 1952, the Altar to the Homeland, the Monument to the Heroic Cadets, was erected at the entrance to Chapultepec forest.

Political necessity more than historical recognition was behind its construction. The first monument dedicated to these cadets had been a small obelisk at the foot of Chapultepec Castle, built between 1880 and 1881 during the governments of Porfirio Díaz and Manuel González. In 1947 U.S. president Harry S. Truman made an official visit to Mexico City and, among other activities, brought a wreath to the Monument to the Heroic Cadets. It was the hundredth anniversary of the war between Mexico and the United States, and there, in Chapultepec, he said: "A century of quarrels is erased with a minute of silence."

His comment fell like a bombshell and unleashed repudiation against the "gringos," who had taken half of Mexico's territory a hundred years earlier. To revive nationalistic fervor, Miguel Alemán's government invented an eight-column news item a few weeks later: during excavations in Chapultepec they had found the remains of the Hero Cadets, sometimes called the Boy Heroes. Nobody believed the news, but Alemán validated it by decree, ordering construction of the new monument, which he launched in 1952 and where he had some remains buried, but it is certain that the authorities perjured themselves when swearing that they were indeed those of the deceased cadets.

Paseo de la Reforma to the west remained unchanged until 1950 when, after the rapture over the Olympic medals won in London in 1948, Alemán ordered construction of an equestrian sports center. When he was informed that in Mexico people used horses for agriculture and not for sport, he changed his mind and opted for construction of an auditorium on Paseo de la Reforma, next to Campo Marte. Thus in 1952 construction of the National Auditorium began. When the building was remodeled in 1989, architect Teodoro González de León said the old auditorium was already "the ugliest building in Mexico, located in the best corner of the country."

In 1952 the Fuente de Petróleos was also dedicated; at that time it occupied the farthest roundabout from Paseo de la Reforma to the west. In 1962 it was modified due to construction of an access road allowing the ring road to pass underneath the fountain that commemorated oil expropriation.

On June 20, 1957, Mexico City suffered a strong earthquake that killed some 700 and injured 2,500. More than the human tragedy, however, the tremor went down in history because the Angel of Independence fell and shattered on the steps of its own monument.

Restoration of the fallen angel took more than a year, and the sculpture took flight again on September 16, 1958, with a different face. The original head could not be restored and today rests in the house of the Counts of Heras y Soto, at 8 Republic of Chile.

After the earthquake of 1957, the Latin American Tower gained worldwide fame. It even won an award for being the tallest building to withstand such force.

Other roundabouts

For almost thirty years, from 1952 to 1980, the view from the Independence Monument to Chapultepec was unbeatable. There were no obstacles, not even skyscrapers, between the angel and Chapultepec Castle, and at the Mississippi River and Seville roundabout, where Diana the Huntress is located today, there was still nothing. During the presidency of José López Portillo (1976–82), however, thanks to the abundance of oil, the government spent lavishly. One of Portillo's great projects was the Cutzamala System, a monumental work to collect and distribute drinking water to the Valley of Mexico. To recognize its importance, in 1980 the government installed the Cutzamala Fountain at the Reforma and Seville roundabout. It immediately received all kinds of criticism and nicknames: "the umbrellas," "the watering cans," "the mushrooms."

It wasn't long before what started as an idea was completed, and sooner rather than later it became abandoned. In 1992 the Cutzamala Fountain was removed to make way for the Diana the Huntress statue.

But be careful, that's not her name; she's the Arrow of the North Star. The work, sculpted by Juan Fernando Olaguíbel, was completed in 1942 when Javier Rojo Gómez, the regent of the Federal District, developed a beautification program for the city. By order of President Ávila Camacho, the work commenced on October 10 of that year. By then it was located at the Reforma and Río Ródano y Lieja roundabout, near its current location at Estela de Luz.

Shortly after its installation, the most conservative sections of the community were outraged that the Diana was naked. The League of Decency protested, putting cloth underwear on her one night. The pressure was so great that the government ordered that the sculptor give her a loincloth. And so she remained until 1967 when she was removed, only to be damaged and recast. In 1992 Manuel Camacho Solís's government decided to rescue her and place her on Paseo de la Reforma.

The equestrian statue of Charles IV, El Caballito, was the most important icon of Paseo de la Reforma for more than a century. It was placed at the start of Bucareli in 1852 and marked the avenue's entrance. But in 1977 Federal District regent Carlos Hank González announced the construction of thirty-four axis roads to streamline vehicular traffic. Axis 1, west Guerrero, Bucareli, determined the fate of the "little horse"; it was necessary to move it so traffic could flow along the axis with no obstacles other than traffic lights.

In May 1979 Tambor, the horse mounted by Charles IV in the sculpture, rode for the last time to the Plaza Tolsá, built between the National Museum of Art and the Palace of Mining, on legendary Calle Tacuba. Thus ended the history of the little horse on Paseo de la Reforma, and with it, the end of an era. In 1992 El Caballito de Sebastián, which was intended to replace the monumental statue of Tolsá, was dedicated, but it never won the people's hearts.

Welcome, Tlāloc

The National Auditorium was the catalyst for important works that in the following years flanked Paseo de la Reforma and created a cultural corridor running from the old entrance to Chapultepec forest to the Petróleos fountain.

History, culture, and the arts took over the paseo. In 1964, the last year of Adolfo López Mateos's six-year term, the Museum of Modern Art and the National Museum of Anthropology were dedicated. Another art museum opened its doors in 1981, the Rufino Tamayo. In that same decade, the Contemporary Art Cultural Center also opened.

Shortly before the inauguration of the National Museum of Anthropology, which housed the most important artifacts of the pre-Hispanic world, on April 16, 1964, people crowded the Reforma to welcome the statue of the rain god, Tlāloc, who had been found in San Miguel Coatlán east of the Valley of Mexico. His new home would be next to Reforma.

Although it continued to rain, people did not move. The god of rain toured the streets of the city atop a twenty-three-meter-long platform equipped with seventy-two Goodrich Euzkadi tires, made especially for the so-called Coatlinchán Operation.

The tour started at 6:15 a.m., when Pedro Ramírez Vázquez, the architect in charge of the operation, gave the order to move the monolith, and continued for nineteen hours until its arrival at the enclosure of Chapultepec at 1:13 a.m. on April 17.

That same year saw the opening of the third stage of Paseo de la Reforma: a 2.6-kilometer extension to the north. Its first roundabout is dedicated to Simón Bolívar, whose statue, unveiled in 1976, was a gift from Venezuela and is a bronze replica of Pietro Canónica's 1934 sculpture.

José de San Martín, another South American liberator, occupies the next roundabout, dedicated in 1973. The penultimate roundabout on Paseo de la Reforma, to the north, is dedicated to another *tlatoani*, Cuitláhuac, the penultimate Aztec king and victor against the Spanish in the 1520 battle called Victorious Night (previously, Night of Sorrows). Of the three roundabouts mentioned, this is the only one initiated by President López Mateos in 1964, the same year the paseo's expansion was completed.

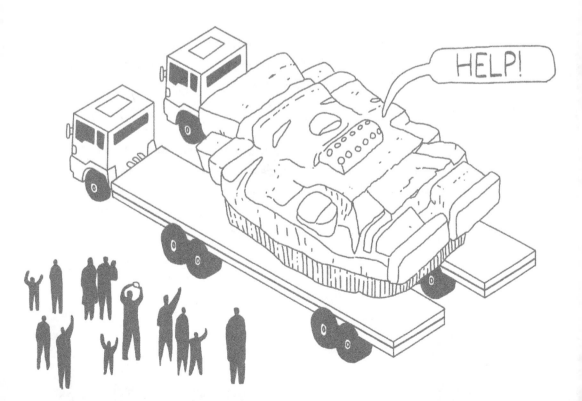

The hour of the insurgents

Avenida de los Insurgentes is another of the capital's most emblematic thoroughfares; at almost thirty kilometers, it crosses the city from north to south and provided access to the states of Hidalgo to the north and Morelos to the south.

The original plans included streets and avenues with different names—Via del Centenario, from downtown to south of the city; and Calle Ramón Guzmán, from downtown to the train station in Buenavista, also known as the road to Laredo; but in 1953 they were unified and renamed Avenida de los Insurgentes.

Some years before the name change, the avenue's sections were incorporated into the surrounding towns. The tranquility of the town of San Ángel, for example, disappeared forever in September 1924, with incorporation of the section ending at Parque de la Bombilla, where four years later President-elect Álvaro Obregón was assassinated in a restaurant.

For San Ángel, the assassination meant transformation. A monument in honor of Obregón was erected on the spot where he lost his hand in 1915 during the battles of the Bajío. It was removed and cremated in 1989. The restaurant Bombilla disappeared, and

Avenida de los Insurgentes was extended south to join with the Cuernavaca highway. In remembrance of the Sonoran leader, in 1931 Villa de San Ángel's name was changed to Villa Álvaro Obregón, and in 1941 it was finally established as the Álvaro Obregón Delegation, today the mayor's office.

The other important road that accelerated urbanization was San Ángel, now Avenida Revolución. In 1929 it ended at La Paz, but it would be extended south with construction of University City in the early 1950s. Thus the convent of Carmen was trapped between two avenues, and San Ángel ceased being a village and became just another neighborhood in the city.

Moctezuma y Cortés

For a long time, Calzada de Tlalpan, one of the oldest avenues on the continent, was known as Calzada de Iztapalapa. The carriageway was built between 1428 and 1440 under Itzcoatl's rule and extended to what is now line 2 of the Ermita subway station. There it headed southeast to reach the manor of Iztapalapa. It connected Tenochtitlan to southern riverside populations and also functioned as a dike, separating the saltwater of Texcoco from the freshwater of Xochimilco and Chalco.

On November 8, 1519, the day Moctezuma and Cortés met for the first time, the Spanish advanced with thousands of Tlaxcalan allies through this causeway toward Tenochtitlan and continued to what is today Avenida Pino Suárez, in the historic center.

Despite the destruction of Tenochtitlan in 1521, its layout was respected and became the natural route to the towns of Coyoacán and Tlalpan. At the end of the nineteenth century, several lines of mule-drawn streetcars came and went that way. Its landscape was rural—fields of crops, ranches, and the occasional building. The streetcar in Tlalpan, however, was reorganized with expansion of the causeway and, over time, incorporated into the city's electric street railway network.

Tlalpan had the curious privilege of being both the State of Mexico (1827–30) and capital of the Republic for a few days (1855). During the viceroyalty period, it was known as San Agustín de las Cuevas. Its patron saint's day is August 28, and during Easter it was the only place in Mexico to allow gambling. Well into the twentieth century, it began to be urbanized, first with a number of hotels where people coming from southern towns could find accommodation quickly. These hotels eventually ended up becoming the places for fleeting love and passion.

The inauguration of subway line 2 in the early 1970s gave impetus to Tlalpan's definitive urban development. Azteca Stadium's opening in 1966, creation of the hospital zone, and extension of the Tlalpan carriageway—Avenida de los Insurgentes and the Periférico ring road—led to Tlalpan's eventual incorporation into the city.

Rivers of asphalt

Since time immemorial, the Valley of Mexico was a lake area, not only because the lake was extensive—so much so that, according to sixteenth-century chronicles, it was impossible to discern its limits—but also because there were about seventy rivers in the region.

Authorities finished engineering the Valley of Mexico rivers in the twentieth century, preferring to enclose rather than protect them. They prioritized asphalt canals over water ones. In the mid-1920s, when vehicular traffic was not a problem, architect Carlos Contreras proposed construction of a ring road surrounding the city, limiting urban growth, and a road uniting the existing neighborhoods. This would be achieved by enclosing three wastewater rivers: La Piedad, Consulado, and Veronica. The idea did not pan out, but the modernity that arrived with Alemán pushed the project forward, and under the leadership of Carlos Lazo the Mixcoac,

Magdalena, Churubusco, and Consulado Rivers were also enclosed; the avenues that carry their names were created above them.

Similarly, construction of the Miguel Alemán viaduct covering La Piedad was encouraged, providing a high-speed artery for many years.

Construction of the Periférico ring road began in the 1960s, and, as happened with other routes, the road grew over time. Today it is nearly ninety kilometers long and runs through Mexico City and part of the State of Mexico. The three sections are Bulevar Manuel Ávila Camacho, from the highway to Querétaro to La Fuente de Petróleos; Avenida Adolfo López Mateos, from this point to the area of Pedregal de San Ángel; and Bulevar Adolfo Ruiz Cortines, from the Pedregal to Chalco.

Although the initial idea was to contain the city, the truth is that countless neighborhoods were created beyond it. The expressway was swallowed up by both the city and traffic. On September 22, 2002, in response to a proposal by Andrés Manuel López Obrador, head of the Federal District government, citizens voted in favor of a second level to help with traffic. Only 9 percent of the electoral roll participated, but the majority were in favor. Never before had such an exercise been carried out in Mexico City.

In 2005 the Metrobus was inaugurated as a fast and effective means of transport through the city's main avenues.

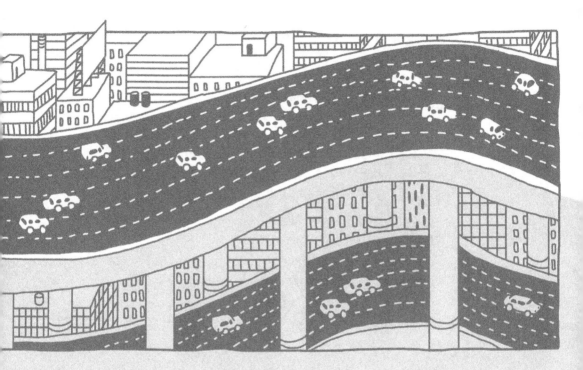

The completed work opened on January 23, 2005, although the road debuted in sections. At every turn there was criticism for favoring cars over public transit; in addition, there was a lack of transparency about the management of resources. But the biggest controversy took place when it was announced, during the government of Marcelo Ebrard, that these would be toll roads. Even so, the project was an immense undertaking and today runs from Cuemanco to Toreo de Cuatro Caminos, where it joins with a section in the State of Mexico, and finally to Cuautitlán.

Roads south

Although University City was one of the great works of Alemán's modernizing impulse, the project had been planned long before his time in office. The university neighborhood, located downtown, had been insufficient to accommodate the university community since the 1940s.

The university chose Pedregal de San Ángel as the site for a new campus in 1943. On September 11, 1946, President Ávila Camacho issued the decree of expropriation of those lands destined for construction of University City.

Resources were provided by Alemán's government, and architects Mario Pani and Enrique del Moral managed the

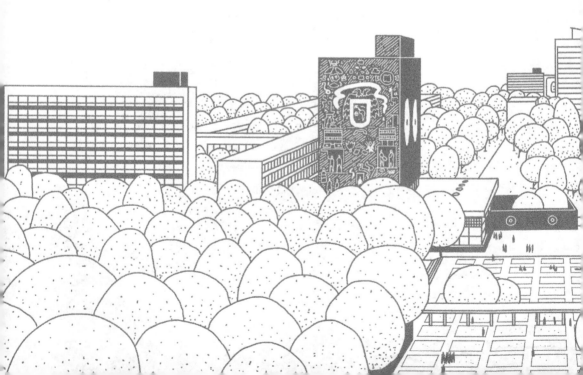

final project. On June 5, 1950, the first stone was laid for the Science Building, which was to be the first of its kind, with the official dedication taking place on November 20, 1952. The move from the city center began in 1953, and classes began in March 1954.

Until the 1950s, the lava field that adjoined Tizapán had been untouchable, maintaining its original appearance as if time had stopped. Modernization put an end to the millenary landscape and merged it with urban development. Construction of University City, the Olympic Stadium, the Pedregal de San Ángel, and Gardens of Pedregal—a new neighborhood—opened the door to in-migration.

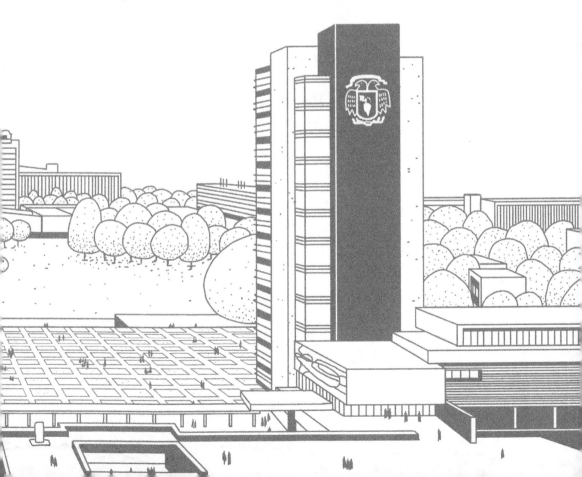

At that time, the concentration of inhabitants in the city's traditional neighborhoods—the Center, Juárez, Roma, Condesa, Cuauhtémoc, Escandón, Tacubaya—caused many people to move toward Tlalpan, San Ángel, Mixcoac, and more remote towns. They already had public services: lighting, sidewalks, drinking water, and drainage. The Tlacopac, San Ángel, and Magdalena Rivers, which still flowed freely in the 1930s, were channeled.

San Ángel, which from its beginnings had comprised the area from Chimalistac to San Jerónimo and La Magdalena, formed a single unit. The city's growth during the second half of the twentieth century ended up fracturing it. It was surrounded by important avenues: Axis 10 South, or Río Magdalena, with what remained separated from the Pedregal; the ring road, Adolfo López Mateos to the west, which demarcated San Jerónimo and Magdalena Contreras; Barranca del Muerto (death cliff) to the north, which established city limits with Mixcoac and Tacubaya; and Revolución to the east.

For years, streetcars were the most popular means of transport. Every hour a train departed from Tizapán, and every half hour another left San Jacinto Plaza for Mexico City and Coyoacán. There were first-class cars, painted yellow, and second-class cars, painted green; hence the name *pericos* (parakeets). The station was in the square—an iron and sheet-metal shed with chairs for passersby waiting for the arrival of transport. A small electric tram connected the Plaza del Carmen with the neighborhood of San Ángel Inn.

Another transportation option was *el rápido*, which started from San Ángel at 7:30 a.m. and passed through

Mixcoac, Tacubaya, and present-day Avenida Chapultepec to stop at Bucareli. The journey lasted thirty minutes. The streetcar was both a means of transportation and a vehicle for sightseeing and amusement. When University City was being built in the 1950s, a streetcar departing from Mixcoac was installed, and many families used it to go around University City with their children.

The trams and the railway disappeared, giving way to the subway. Buses, minibuses, and cabs soon replaced the nineteenth-century carriages and buses. The paradox of progress, however, is that with the development of routes in the nineteenth and early twentieth centuries, which reduced travel time between Mexico City and San Ángel, traffic problems meant the return of hours-long trips similar to the ones made by the inhabitants of New Spanish Mexico.

The subway

On September 4, 1969, President Gustavo Díaz Ordaz and Federal District regent Alfonso Corona del Rosal inaugurated the Collective Subway Transportation System, so named in reference to the metropolitan train between the Chapultepec and Zaragoza stations.

During the second half of the twentieth century, Mexico City suffered from serious traffic congestion, especially downtown. In 1958 engineer Bernardo Quintana, a

founder of Mexican Civil Engineers, presented the metro project to Federal District authorities, but they rejected it due to high costs. When the project was re-presented during Díaz Ordaz's presidency, he approved it thanks to credit obtained from the French government, and construction began in June 1967.

The Metro is the capital's most complex civil engineering project, with eleven lines in operation, 175 stations, more than 14,000 workers, and some 4.2 million daily users. Each line is distinguished by a color and station icon that references its location, toponymy, and the history of its direction.

Lines 1, 2, and 3 were opened by Díaz Ordaz; lines 4 and 5, by José López Portillo; lines 6, 7, and 9, by Miguel de la Madrid; lines 8 and A, by Carlos Salinas de Gortari; and line B, by Ernesto Zedillo. Line 12, the last to open, had many scandals and corruption problems. It began operation in 2012 and suffered a terrible accident in 2021.

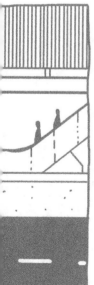

In 2021 a new form of electric transport was launched: the cable bus. There are services from Indios Verdes to Cuautepec; from Santa Martha to Constitución of 1917; and above Chapultepec.

TU
RU
RU

Taking the Metro is an experience that is both decipherable and indecipherable; it is, on one hand, the miracle of accommodation, and, on the other hand, the exact idea of how one feels in Mexico City.

— Carlos Monsiváis

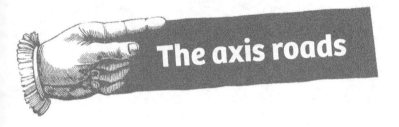

The axis roads

In 1978 much of the city was leveled by an earthquake. Buildings were demolished, and entire blocks lay in rubble, with ditches, dirt, and dust all over the city. These were the ravages of one of the most important public works of the second half of the twentieth century: the axis roads.

There were workers everywhere and signposts, closed avenues, and insufferable traffic, all in the interest of improving automobile traffic in the capital. The project had been supported by López Portillo, but the principal proponent, and the person in charge of carrying it out, was none other than Carlos Hank González, head of the Federal District during the 1976–82 term.

> When making the axis road, the citizens got angry. They hated me and insulted Hank González . . . and his mother. It was terrible! But it had to be done, and people were right to complain. . . . Materially, I had to destroy the city so that later they would allow me to rebuild it, as was done. I remember that it was a time of jokes: that I was no longer Hank González but "Zanjas Viales" (road digger); many insults, many offenses.
>
> — Carlos Hank González,
> interview in *La Jornada*, June 26, 1999

EJE
CENTRAL

TROLE

REP. DE CUBA

The time was ripe for construction. The government had just discovered the Cantarell oilfield and had money to spend, with plenty of hands to spend it. On June 23, 1979, the president and regent inaugurated the first fifteen half-opened axis roads, which amounted to 133 kilometers. Some were unfinished, and others had only a few lanes in operation. Motorists were not aware of them until Monday, June 25, when confusion ensued. The axis roads crossing Avenida de los Insurgentes were almost deserted. Motorists got used to the new roads slowly, continuing to drive on the same streets they had been using for more than a year. López Portillo himself had his doubts about the project, but he let Hank González do it.

> Last Saturday I christened the famous axis roads, here in the Federal District. What a scandal! They're here. I hope they work and justify their expense and prestige. Hank really took a gamble. Now he will reap the benefits.
>
> — José López Portillo

255

In the 1960s the capital doubled in size. The surrounding towns of Tacubaya, San Ángel, Tizapán, Tlalpan, and Coyoacán had already become part of the city, and to address the increasing number of cars, huge avenues like Universidad and Revolución were opened. From that point on, the capital transformed radically: it lost its rural aspect as the population almost tripled; trucks and automobiles became a daily part of the urban landscape; and department stores like Sears and Woolworths began to appear.

The construction of striking multifamily houses and the creation of neighborhoods such as Del Valle, Narvarte, and Satellite City, within the State of Mexico but linked to the city by the Periférico ring road, symbolized the growth of the middle-class.

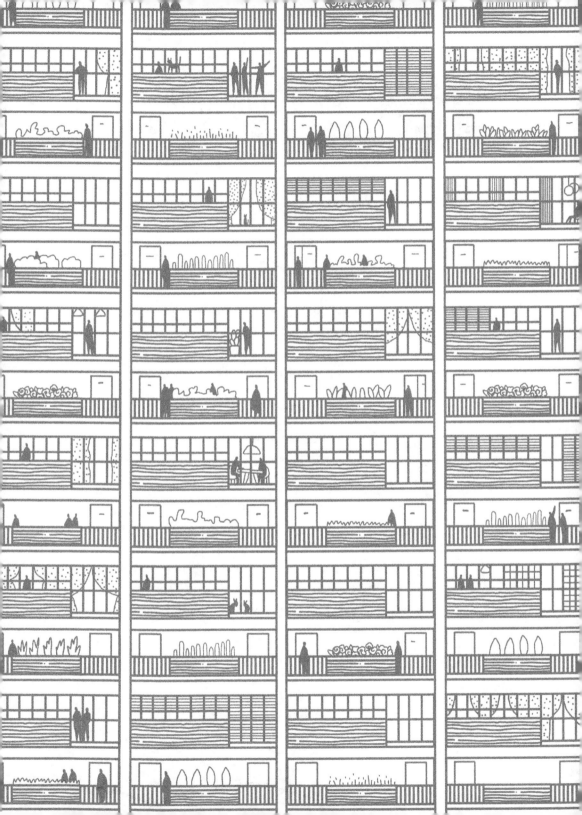

Sports and events

The twentieth century was also the century of sporting venues. The Basque ball game, boxing, wrestling, bullfighting, baseball, soccer, and auto racing became popular among the public.

On May 10, 1929, the Frontón México opened, an art deco–style "ball palace" located next to the unfinished structure of what in 1938 would be the Monument to the Revolution.

It was no surprise to anyone that the Basque ball game, in its different forms—paleta, jai alai, ski lift, and solid rubber paddle—had such a spectacular venue. The game's tradition dates to colonial times, when gambling among Spaniards living in Mexico, and more than a few creoles, was part of daily entertainment. The taste for the game managed to transcend eras and the direst circumstances, and Frontón México opened its doors in a new era of peace and stability.

Toward the mid-twentieth century, some still held a nostalgia for the daily life of Díaz's time. The Jockey Club, whose headquarters were in the House of Tiles, had disappeared, but many generals retained a certain fascination for horses. The revolution had been conceived on the back of a sorrel or a dapple at full gallop.

During Manuel Ávila Camacho's six-year term (1940–46), racetracks such as Peralvillo, Indianilla, and that of the Condesa neighborhood disappeared. But at the insistence of businessman Bruno Pagliai and with support of the president, whose weakness was horses, the Hipódromo de las Américas was built in Lomas de Sotelo. It was the first time this type of

In the nineteenth century's early days of cycling, racetracks were used for bike races. The hippodrome was dedicated on March 6, 1943, and has been a social meeting place for horse racing fans ever since.

structure had been built outside the city center, six kilometers away.

Like horse racing, bullfighting found a new impetus in the mid-twentieth century. In the early 1940s the Plaza de Toros in the Condesa—called El Toreo, from the Porfirian period—still occupied the present-day streets of Durango, Salamanca, Valladolid, and Colima. It was inaugurated in 1907, with a capacity for twenty-five thousand. With demolition of the hippodrome and construction of the new neighborhood, however, its presence was unpopular in the area. The site it had occupied was used to build a chain store, the Palacio de Hierro, at the end of the 1940s.

Today bullfighting is no longer a popular spectacle. In 2022 a judge definitively suspended bullfighting in Plaza México.

Construction of Plaza de Toros México, or simply Plaza México, was part of a larger project to build Sports City, a sports complex with a football stadium, swimming pools, a fronton, a boxing and wrestling arena, cinemas, and restaurants. The project was businessman Neguib Simón Jalife's idea; he wanted to build it on land once occupied by San Carlos Ranch.

On April 28, 1944, Javier Rojo Gómez, the city's regent, laid Sports City's first stone. Construction, of course, ran up against reality, and in the absence of investors Jalife was only able to build the bullring and the Olympic stadium, today's Estadio Azul.

The bullring opened on February 5 of that year. In its first lineup were Luis "The Soldier" Castro, Manuel Rodríguez Manolete, and Luis Procuna with San Mateo bulls.

As in other times, Plaza México allowed for different shows and has hosted rock and other popular music concerts. It has also served as the stage for the opera *Carmen*, political campaign closures, such as that of Felipe Calderón in 2006, and stunt motorcycle demonstrations like the Red Bull X-Fighters.

The day after the inaugural bullfight at Plaza México, on February 6, 1946, it was the stadium's turn. It opened its doors to a football game between National University and the Harriers of the Military College, with the university team winning.

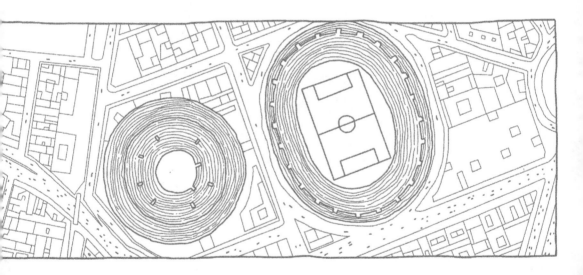

The University Stadium of University City got off to an epic start. With less than a minute to play in the Poly–University classic and Polytechnic in the lead, their fans began to light torches as a sign of victory. It was November 20, 1952, and the visiting team's victory seemed imminent, but with a few seconds left University's running back, Juan Romero, received the ball and, with an extraordinary block by Alfonso "The Fiend" García, managed to reach the end zone to leave the scoreboard 20–19 in University's favor. The crowd went wild. There was no better way to celebrate the stadium's inauguration.

Although it had been built for American football, over time the stadium became the home of the Pumas de la Universidad soccer team, and today the people of the Noche Buena neighborhood associate it with soccer. The stadium was remodeled to host the 1968 Olympic Games, and in 1978 it hosted the first NFL game outside the United States, with the New Orleans Saints facing off against the Philadelphia Eagles. It was also a World Cup stadium in 1986 and has been the venue for other international competitions.

The most famous of the sporting venues is Estadio Azteca. The stadium, designed by architects Pedro Ramírez Vázquez and Rafael Mijares, was built on Santa Úrsula communal land on the Tlalpan carriageway. It was dedicated on May 29, 1966, by Díaz Ordaz, accompanied by city regent Ernesto P. Uruchurtu; Stanley Ross, president of FIFA; businessman Emilio Azcárraga

Milmo; and the presidents of the América, Atlante, and Necaxa soccer clubs.

In their first encounter, the Colossus of Santa Úrsula hosted the teams of América and Torin. The game ended in a 2–2 draw. The first goal was scored by América player Arlindo dos Santos.

The stadium has hosted the 1970 and 1986 World Cups, in which Pelé (1970) and Diego Maradona (1986) reached the pinnacle of soccer glory, the latter with his so-called Hand of God goal.

It has also hosted concerts, including pop group Menudo in 1983, which filled the stadium to capacity and which the press said was "the night the Azteca sang"; five Michael Jackson concerts, which brought together half a million people; and Elton John, Luis Miguel, U2, NSYNC, Bronco, Juan Gabriel, and Gloria Estefan. It has also been the venue of several NFL games, boxing matches such as the one featuring Julio César Chávez in the mid-1990s, and Pope John Paul II's visit in 1999.

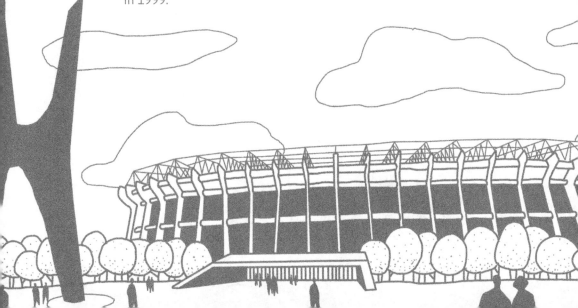

The Department of Social Security's Sports Park, situated on the Piedad viaduct and the Cuauhtémoc axis road, was home to the capital's two baseball teams, the Red Devils and Tigers, from its opening in 1955.

Although it was the city's biggest baseball arena, in 1985 it served as the venue where bodies of the victims of the terrible earthquake of September 19 were taken. The park's history ended on June 1, 2000, with the last game between the Tigers and the Devils, which the latter won.

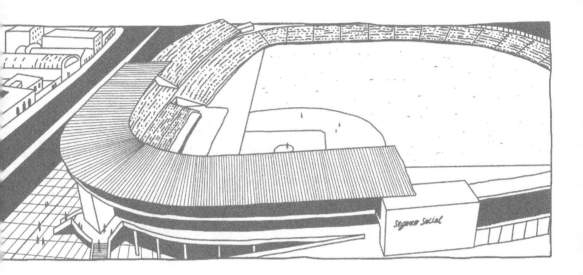

It was demolished to make way for a shopping center that reclaimed the site's original name, Delta Park. Baseball and its fans had to move a few kilometers to the city's east, and the Mexican league's matches resumed in the Foro Sol sports and entertainment center on June 2, 2000.

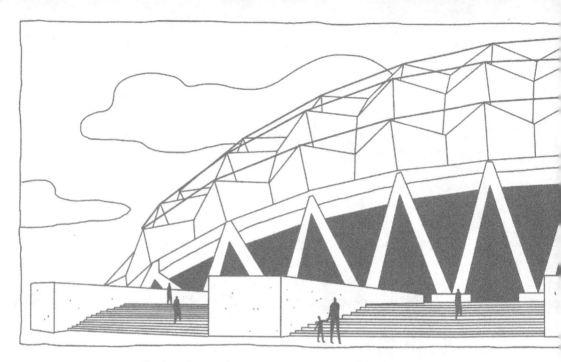

During the Porfiriate's last years, people often gathered on the sidewalks of Paseo de la Reforma or went to the racetracks to enjoy the first automobile races, but it wasn't until 1959 that the city had its own autodrome. The Autódromo Hermanos Rodríguez, named in honor of notable drivers Pedro and Ricardo Rodríguez, opened on December 20, 1959, with the Mexico City 500 Kilometers, in a race lasting four hours and forty-seven minutes with an average vehicle speed of 104 kilometers per hour. The autodrome's inauguration generated such interest that it attracted a hundred thousand people.

In 1962 a Formula 1 grand prix was held in the city for the first time, but the race did not count toward the championship score. The autodrome was considered an official circuit for the regular race calendar from 1963 to 1970, from 1986 to 1992, and from 2015 to date.

In 1993 the enclosure's banked curve was transformed for several massive concerts, including Madonna, Paul McCartney, Pink Floyd, and the Rolling Stones. This proved so successful that entrepreneurs decided to build a proper forum, and in October 1997 the Foro Sol was dedicated with a monster trucks–motocross exhibition and a David Bowie concert. The Foro Sol was built on the site of the 1950s Magdalena Mixhuca Sports City.

The Palacio de los Deportes was built opposite the racetrack for the 1968 Olympic Games. It has also been used for performances of *Aida* and other operas as well as ballets like Maurice Béjart's Ballet of the Twentieth Century company, which performed at the opening of the enclosure on October 8, 1968, in the middle of the Olympic Games, trade shows, fairs, and concerts.

Pollution

Along with constant flooding, the city had to face the problems of air pollution and vehicular traffic. "It will be temporary," they said. "It will help improve air quality," they said. "It will only apply in winter," they said. And so, starting in November 1989, residents of Mexico City were introduced to the Hoy no circula (no driving today) program and the apocalyptic meaning of vehicle verification. Residents detested them, repudiated them, kicked and screamed and learned to live with them.

Pollution had been increasing since the early 1980s. In 1982 Imeca, the Metropolitan Air Quality Index, was created to measure the concentration of pollutants in the air breathed by the capital's inhabitants. Whenever it was mentioned in the media from 1986 onward, people began to think and talk about thermal inversions, and at the same time the government began making plans to combat the environmental exigency.

The efforts were insufficient, however, and the first results of the car-free day were disconcerting: air quality did not improve, but traffic did, which was not insignificant. Gasoline consumption also decreased, which was also not negligible because it affected the government's coffers.

Months later the pollution problem worsened, and in 1990 the government of Mexico City announced that the Hoy no circula program would be applied year-round.

Mexico City today

In 2021 Mexico City turned five hundred: five centuries, twenty generations, and thousands of stories. With a little more than nine million inhabitants plus many others, mainly from the states of Mexico, Morelos, and Hidalgo, the capital is a varied, colorful, and entertaining megalopolis.

Great political and social transformations have had their origin or climax there. The capital is a liberal city, the first to approve the legal termination of pregnancy, to allow marriage equality between people of the same sex, to grant to its inhabitants the right

to elect their own governors in 1997. It is also the city with the most unusual Guinness World Records: in 2009, for the most kisses at one time (42,224 people kissed in the Zócalo); and in 2011, for Zombie Walk Mexico City (9,806 people dressed as zombies walked down its avenues). The capital managed to break the record for the most people dancing at one time, in 2009 to Michael Jackson's "Thriller." Mexico City also erected the tallest Christmas tree in the world, holds the record for the largest number of mariachis playing at one time, and, in October 2009, obtained the record for the largest number of people looking at the moon through telescopes at one time.

Although the capital had been known, from 1824 onward, as the Federal District, it was changed through a constitutional reform, and as of January 30, 2016, the capital's official name became Mexico City, less than two hundred years after the Federal District formation.

Each of the city's neighborhoods, its streets, its corners, tells its own story—La Portales with its famous California Dancing Club; Santa María La Ribera with its Moorish kiosk; the tobacco company with the Monument to the Revolution; Zona Rosa (the pink zone), because she was too shy to be red and too bold to be white, with her centers such as the Señorial, the Jacarandas Hall, the Patio, and the Marrakesh complex; Tacuba, where Goyo Cárdenas scandalized the capital's inhabitants with his murders in the 1940s; La Roma with Avenida Álvaro Obregón; Balbuena Garden, where the history of aviation in Mexico was born; Churubusco, where the Cineteca once was; the Anzures, where the famous Camino Real was built. One could go on, listing hundreds of neighborhoods defined by their own daily life.

Mexico City was home to some of the great protagonists of history, both nationally and internationally. In the twentieth century it was known by John F. Kenne-

dy and his wife, Jacqueline Bouvier; Charles de Gaulle; Salvador Allende; Queen Elizabeth II of England; Pope John Paul II and his successors; Fidel Castro; Che Guevara; kings of Spain; Harry S. Truman; the astronauts who landed on the moon in 1969 (Armstrong, Aldrin, and Collins); sportsmen such as Platini, Senna, and Prost; and artists such as Marilyn Monroe, Paul McCartney, and Madonna, among many others.

It is a city that has been transformed in every era, in every century, and in every circumstance. It is a city where sushi became Mexicanized with the famous restaurant Sushito, the time of Carlos & Charlies, the flash taco, and Tizoncito. It has changed with the times, going from nightclubs to the discotheques of the 1980s and 1990s, including the Magic Circus, the News, the Vandasha, La Boom, the Premier, Rockoti-tlán, the Bulldog, and the Jubilee.

It is the city where more than a million people queued to see the giant panda born in Chapultepec Zoo in 1981 or met Cornelius the Dragon of Adventure Kingdom; where they applauded Keiko, the killer whale who put on a show every day; or got dizzy in Uncle Chueco's Cabin or went on the Krakatoa Canoe and, if they were more adventurous, went on the famous roller coaster at the Chapultepec Fair, which was a challenge of bravery because it always seemed at risk of falling down.

It is a city that has suffered great tragedies such as the 1985 earthquake, which devastated a large part of the capital and left ten thousand dead on September 19, a date on which, incredibly, the natural phenomenon was repeated thirty-two years later in 2017. Between one tremor and another, the people of the capital are aware that they inhabit a city where earthquakes take place every day. The new generations grew up listening to the seismic alert, participating in drills, and focusing on prevention, which ensured that the 2017 earthquake wasn't so bloody and showed the *chilanga* solidarity that always arises in the face of tragedy.

Recommended Reading

Alamán, Lucas. *Historia de México*. 5 vols. Mexico City: FCE, 1985.

Almonte, Juan Nepomuceno. *Guía de forasteros y repertorio de conocimientos útiles*. Mexico City: Instituto Mora, 1997.

Álvarez, José María. *Añoranzas. El México que fue mi Colegio Militar*. Mexico City: Imprenta Ocampo, 1948.

Calderón de la Barca, Madame. *Life in Mexico, During a Residency of Two Years in That Country*. London: Chapman & Hall, 1843.

Castorena y Ursúa, Juan Ignacio de, and Juan Francisco Sahagún de Arévalo Ladrón de Guevara. *Gacetas de México, 1722–1748*. Mexico City: SEP, 1949.

Durán, Fray Diego. *The History of the Indies of New Spain*. Norman: University of Oklahoma Press, 1994.

García Cubas, Antonio. *El libro de mis recuerdos*. Mexico City: Patria, 1969.

González Obregón, Luis. *Las calles de México*. Mexico City: Porrúa, 1995 / *The Streets of Mexico*. Victoria, Australia: Hassell Street Press, 2021.

———. *México viejo*. Mexico City: Alianza Editorial, 1997.

Guijo, Gregorio M. de. *Diario 1648–1664*. 2 vols. Mexico City: Porrúa, 1986.

Humboldt, Alexander von. *A Political Essay on the Kingdom of New Spain*. 2 vols. Chicago: University of Chicago Press, 2019.

Marroquí, José María. *La Ciudad de México*. 3 vols. Edited by Jesús Medina. Mexico City: J. Medina, 1969.

Nacif Mina, Jorge. *La policía en la historia de la Ciudad de México, 1524–1928*. Mexico City: DDF/Socicultur, 1986.

Olavarría y Ferrari, Enrique de. *Reseña histórica del teatro en México, 1538–1911*. Mexico City: Porrúa, 1961.

Ramos i Duarte, Feliz. *Diccionario de curiosidades históricas, geográficas, hierográficas, cronológicas de la república mexicana*. Mexico City: Imprenta de Eduardo Dublán, 1899.

Rivera Cambas, Manuel. *México pintoresco, artístico y monumental*. Mexico City: Editorial del Valle de México, 1985.

Robles, Antonio de. *Diario de sucesos notables, 1665–1703*. 3 vols. Mexico City: Porrúa, 1972.

Sedano, Francisco. *Noticias de México*. Mexico City: DDF / Colección Metropolitana, 1974.

Torquemada, Fray Juan de. *Handbook of Middle American Indians*. Austin: University of Texas Press, 1973.

Tovar de Teresa, Guillermo. *The City of Palaces: Chronicle of a Lost Heritage*. Mexico City: Vuelta, 1990.

Valle-Arizpe, Artemio de. *Calle vieja y calle nueva*. Mexico City: Diana, 1997.

———. *Obras completas*. Mexico City: Libreros Mexicanos Unidos, 1960.

Mexico City is five hundred years old;
half a millennium of stories
and those yet to be written, and there is a
maxim that seems to be a prophecy:
"As long as the world exists, the fame and glory
of Mexico-Tenochtitlan will never end."

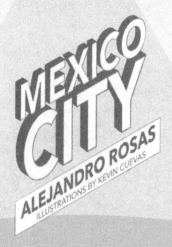

MEXICO CITY

ALEJANDRO ROSAS
ILLUSTRATIONS BY KEVIN CUEVAS

Printed in the USA
CPSIA information can be obtained
at www.ICGtesting.com
JSHW050356210923
48751JS00003B/3